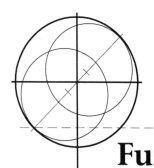

Bringing the Future into Focus

An Introduction to
the Progressive
Christian Worldview

Harold R. Eberle

Winepress Publishing
Yakima, Washington

Bringing the Future into Focus
An Introduction to the Progressive Christian Worldview

© 2002 by Harold R. Eberle
First Printing, June 2002

Winepress Publishing
P.O. Box 10653
Yakima, WA 98909-1653
(509) 248-5837
www.winepress.org
winepress@nwinfo.net

ISBN 1-882523-20-2
Cover by Paul Jones

Printed in the United States of America

Credits and Thanks

Several Bible teachers, pastors, and friends read through the manuscript of this book, adding their insights and comments. Although no one agrees with me 100%, they all sharpened my thinking and helped me communicate my beliefs more clearly. Since they each labored through these pages and left their marks herein, they deserve special mention: Joe Johnson, Joshua Eberle, Henk and Marjolein van Diest, Pastor Bob Congdon, John Alcamo, Pastor Ron Thomasson, Jane Johnson, Dr. Daniel Juster, Pastor Jeff Ecklund, R.D. Smith, Pastor Mike Lightfoot, Pastor Martin Trench, Apostle Bruce Latshaw, and Dr. Winn Griffin,

James Bryson helped me refine my style of writing and Annette Bradley is my final editor.

Four friends repeatedly challenged me in my theological beliefs and that initially stirred me to study these subjects for myself. They deserve recognition for their pioneering spirit and persistence: Apostle Ted Hansen, Pastor Mike Lightfoot, Bible Teacher Stan Newton, and Pastor Martin Trench.

Thanks to all of you.

About the Author

While pastoring a congregation in the northwestern United States, Harold R. Eberle had a visitation from God which convinced him that the Church will rise in glory, unity, and maturity before the return of our Lord Jesus. Mr. Eberle then began to speak and minister to the larger Body of Christ. Since 1986, he has been traveling and ministering at Christian gatherings, leadership conferences, and churches of many different doctrinal persuasions. He now is engaged in a worldwide teaching ministry.

Among his works, he has founded and oversees several Bible Colleges in Africa. He has a goal of establishing 50 colleges in developing nations across the world.

He lives in Yakima, Washington, with his wife Linda. God has blessed them with three children. Yakima also serves as home base for the ministry operations, which include the oversight of Winepress Ministries and Winepress Publishing.

A prolific author, Mr. Eberle has written numerous books, several of which have been translated in other languages and distributed worldwide. His primary focus is upon preparing the Church for a mighty awakening. He is passionately in love with the Church and believes that God currently is fitly framing the people of God into a Temple in which He can dwell. The call you often will hear from his heart is, "God is coming to Earth!"

Table of Contents

Introduction

Too many Christians have built their understanding of the Bible, the world, history, and the future upon a perception which is robbing them of faith, hope, and love. It is robbing them of faith because they have accepted the lie that the Church is impotent and will remain helpless until Jesus returns. Their perception is stealing their hope because they see the Church as a cumbersome ark moving through an ocean of evil. They focus on the myth that Satan is in control of this world, rather than recognizing that Jesus is Lord and Satan already has been defeated. They think that they love people, but in reality, they live with abiding suspicions that their neighbor, the government, the church across town, Roman Catholics, the financial giants, Russia, China, and the Islamic world soon will be used by the Antichrist to deceive all those who are unaware.

Whether or not you realize it, you have been influenced by such lies. They permeate modern Protestant Christianity. Whether or not you accept them as true, they still have influenced the overall picture you now have in your mind concerning the passing of time and how the future will unfold.

Bringing the Future into Focus

I am going to hold up a mirror so you can see what is going on within your own thought processes. Then I will refocus the image so you can form a more accurate view of yourself and the future.

I will be using the term "progressive worldview" to describe the Christian worldview which I believe is the most biblically accurate. Many Christian teachers use this term in referring to smaller, distinct areas of life and experience. I am applying it to our whole worldview. Today a significant portion of the Church thinks along these same lines, but I am unaware of other teachers who use the term "progressive" in such a broad sense as I do. I am hoping it will ring true in the hearts of many and quickly catch on.

My use of the term "progressive worldview" should not be confused with how a certain smaller modern sect uses this term in order to push Christians into more liberal positions. The Progressive Christian Worldview which I am offering is a solid biblically-based view of the Bible, history, and the future.

Escaping Frenzied Christianity

You and I recently have experienced one of the greatest scams in the history of Christianity. Over \$1 billion were drained from the pockets of the Body of Christ—and no one has been held accountable! We have heard no public apology and most Christians are unaware that it even happened to them.

Just before the dawn of this millennium, people were stirred into a frenzy concerning the scare of Y2K. People all over the world were affected, but sincere Christians were the most susceptible and American Christians were hit the worst. They more than any other people diverted tens of millions of dollars into the purchase of food, storage containers, flashlights, and generators. They held their breath as the clock approached the midnight hour of the last millennium.

Then it happened—nothing.

It is not just the financial loss that disturbs me. It is deeper. It is the fact that Christians could be so easily swept into such fear. They reasoned that God needed to cause some catastrophic event in order to awaken people to revival or to usher in the return of Jesus Christ. Many actually wanted God to cause an economic crash. They hoped that He would send the world into chaos. They expected God to have His day of vengeance. They thought God was as frustrated with the world as they were and that, finally, He was going to do something about it.

Bringing the Future into Focus

Does anyone dare admit our mistake? Or shall we hide our heads in the sand and pretend that we did not err? Perhaps we should pray that God gets 'em next time.

Christians are supposed to be wise, yet they certainly missed it with the Y2K fiasco. They turned out to be the most gullible and ignorant of all people. Worst of all, they were estranged from the heart and plan of God, as I will show later.

This has happened more than once. Every few years, various groups of Christians catch the "Endtime Madness disease."

In some ways, it is similar to "Mad Cow Disease." When my wife and I were traveling in England at the height of the last outbreak, cattle and sheep owners were going to great extent to stop the spread of this plague. Tens of thousands of livestock were put to death. As we traveled through England, we noticed many areas that were unaffected. In still other areas, the livestock were all dead.

In similar fashion, the disease of Endtime Madness seems to incubate and spread most successfully in certain parts of the world. As I travel and speak in many nations, I notice that Christians in my own home country of America are among the most susceptible. Indeed, the closer I get to Southern California or certain other locations, the more often I find Christians seriously infected.

Endtime Madness leads to foolish behavior. The Bible tells us that without a vision people perish (Prov. 29:18). If they have no vision beyond the soon return of our Lord, then they get hit by a form of mental paralysis. Without realizing it, parents care less for their children's education. Long-range financial planning seems less significant, even vain. Businesspeople get out of bed Monday morning still dazed by the preacher's Sunday message concerning the imminent end of this world.

Christians infected by Endtime Madness stop reading their Bibles and spend their "devotional times" reading books which focus on the great trials that lie ahead of us. They fill their minds with how bad the world is and how everything is getting worse. They hold to the assurance that Jesus soon will return to rescue us, and that message becomes the standard by which every minister is evaluated. Every time they hear a minister preach, they think that he or she missed God if the message was not centered on endtimes or at least ended with a reminder that Jesus Christ soon will return to rescue us out of the increasing mess of humanity.

Endtime Madness is a symptom of a limited intellectual and biblically-balanced diet. Christians who expose themselves to only one way of thinking and isolate themselves from what the rest of the Body of Christ believes soon form the distorted perspective of this disease.

I can compare it with a food craze which has recently taken hold of many in my home town. A certain type of doughnuts, called *Krispy Kremes,* have become very popular. I can testify why because I, too, have had them melt in my mouth for a quick delight. I also know that if you eat four or more Krispy Kreme doughnuts and wash them down with coffee, you will have plenty of energy to accomplish the work ahead of you—at least for the next two hours.

Yet, if you eat only Krispy Kremes, you are going to be sick. Eventually it will show on your body; it will show in your mind. More healthy foods will seem unappealing and even boring.

Similarly, Christians who accumulate endtime books and saturate their minds and hearts with the words of endtime televangelists develop an unhealthy form of Christianity. They don't know they are sick because each message they hear sounds so important, so urgent, so stimulating. An evangelist can spread his frenzy and motivate the listeners to act quickly, responding to his every appeal. However, that level cannot be maintained long term. The push of the televangelist does not always match God's desires for the individual listener, nor for his family, business, finances, future, or ministry.

Just before the opening of the new millennium, I was asked to write a book on the soon-coming end of the world. A major publisher of Christian books assured me that he could sell thousands if I just hurried so he could get them into the Christian bookstores. I didn't write it. I never believed anything significant was going to happen with Y2K, nor do I believe that Endtime Madness produces healthy Christianity in the Church.

Most of the Christian leaders with whom I have been relating over the last few years have been waiting eagerly for this millennium to dawn. Before that crossover date, Christians' minds were permeated with fear that God was about to end it all. We knew we could not fight the massive bombardment of end-time propaganda. It was impossible back then to introduce successfully a different, more positive way of thinking. Yet now we all have crossed the millennial line and we are still here. Many are lifting their eyes to look further down the road. They are disillusioned with date-setting preachers. They are questioning the wisdom of short-term planning. They are beginning to question whether God may have a plan for this world—other than its soon destruction.

I want to show you a different way of thinking—a more sane way of thinking. In the process, I hope to inoculate you against Endtime Madness. More important, I want to offer you a different worldview—a worldview which is more healthy and biblical.

By "worldview," I am referring to the way in which a person looks at life, society, Creation, and the whole world as it advances throughout history and into the future.

I need to take you on a journey to show you how your present worldview developed and where it went wrong. This will require some labor on both your and my part. We must glance back at history and consider the influences which have formed our present thought patterns. We must confront our own ways of thinking and correct them where they have gone askew.

If you will enter into this process with me, you will be left with a more optimistic worldview. You will obtain a clearer picture of God's plan for humanity and His heart toward us right now. You will recognize His hand sovereignly moving in the nations across the world. You will have hope where once you had fear.

Bringing the Future into Focus

If you allow me the privilege of challenging your present thought patterns, you will be left with a more sane basis on which to govern your life. You will be wiser in making daily decisions, such as what goals to set for your children, where to invest your finances, how your business can become more successful, what ministries God will be blessing in the coming years, and what you should be planning for your future.

Please walk this path with me. It will take some time, but when the future comes into focus, you will realize how important and fruitful this journey will have been for your own life.

 **The Evangelical Worldview**

I am going to explain to you how Evangelical Christians think.

When I use the term "Evangelical," I am referring to Christians (including myself) who believe the Bible to be the inspired Word of God and hence have as a central doctrine the belief that every person must believe in Jesus Christ to have their sins forgiven and live eternally with God.* This includes Pentecostals and Charismatics.

Evangelicals share a worldview which looks over the course of time and sees four major events: Creation, the Fall of Humanity, Redemption, and the Consummation. Summarizing this viewpoint, God's perfect will was manifested in Creation, with humans put in charge of the Earth. Everything was created good. When Adam and Eve sinned, not only did evil come into the world, but the whole of Creation was corrupted. Then God sent Jesus to redeem humankind, but the fullness of His redemption will not be realized until the final judgment, when every person will be sent to heaven or hell eternally.

During the Protestant Reformation leaders clearly defined this worldview. It lies at the foundation of all

---

* Typically the older mainline denominations, such as Roman Catholic, Orthodox, Lutheran, and Episcopal, are not considered Evangelical, although many members within these denominations are Evangelical in their beliefs.

Bringing the Future into Focus

Christianity, yet it became crystallized in the wake of the Reformation as Reformed Theology was developed.

A significant point of this worldview is that humankind is seen as being on a downward slide. Ever since the Fall, people have been totally helpless, entirely dependent upon God to redeem them through our Lord Jesus Christ.

The Worldview of Reformed Theology

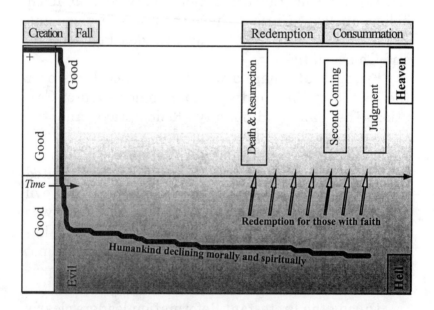

Modern Evangelicals share this basic understanding, but then various groups further develop it in their own unique ways. They build upon the foundation, adding historic events and ways of interpreting those events.

The Evangelical Worldview

We will examine three resulting worldviews. They are called: *dispensational, restorational,* and *progressive.* These are three distinct ways in which Evangelical Christians today view the overall workings of God. As we look at each of these worldviews, we will see how they determine much concerning what a group of Christians believes and does. After defining and comparing them, we will see why the progressive worldview is more helpful, fruitful, optimistic, and biblically accurate.

With that worldview, you will get a new perspective of how the future will unfold.

The Dispensational Worldview

Many Evangelical Christians and entire denominations have a *dispensational* way of looking at the Bible, history, and the future. They identify the various covenants God made with humankind and teach that God dealt with people differently during each time period (or each dispensation) when that specific covenant was valid,

Dispensationalists divide the Old Testament into several periods:

- The Creation to the Fall of humanity
- The Fall to Noah
- Noah to Abraham
- Abraham to Moses
- Moses to David
- David to the exile of the Jewish nation (or the end of the Old Testament)

The New Testament typically is broken into the time period during which Jesus walked the Earth and the period during which the early Church was being established.

Then follows the "Church Age" (sometimes called the Age of Grace) which extends into the present. After this Church Age, they envision a dispensation of endtime judgments, then a 1,000-year reign of Jesus on the Earth, and finally the dispensation of eternity.

Bringing the Future into Focus

Certain dispensational groups identify different or additional dispensations, but all of them tend to see the workings of God in clear distinct blocks of time.*

The Advancement of Time in the Mind of the Dispensational Christian

(The spacings between the lines in the diagram do not correspond with actual time lapsed within a dispensation.)

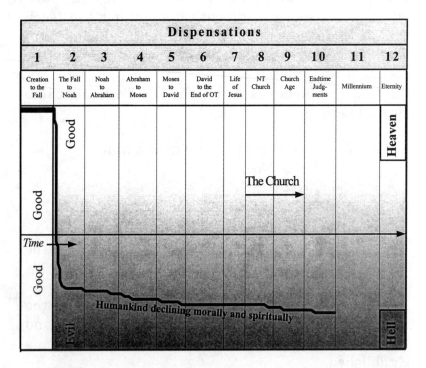

Dispensations											
1	**2**	**3**	**4**	**5**	**6**	**7**	**8**	**9**	**10**	**11**	**12**
Creation to the Fall	The Fall to Noah	Noah to Abraham	Abraham to Moses	Moses to David	David to the End of OT	Life of Jesus	NT Church	Church Age	Endtime Judgments	Millennium	Eternity

---

* A large percentage of modern dispensationalists envision seven dispensations rather than twelve. To see this number you can use the diagram above and combine dispensations 5 and 6; also 7, 8, and 9. They see the Millennium as the seventh and final dispensation; eternity is not included as a dispensation.

Thinking in such clear-cut time periods helps dispensational Christians explain the changes they see in God's dealings with humankind throughout history. It also explains to present-day Christians why they do not have to submit to the Mosaic Law and the religious ceremonies of the Jewish people. The dispensationalist does not have to wrestle with how the workings of God in one period apply to people in another period.

Unfortunately, this "benefit" also allows people a convenient way to reject certain truths which have been revealed in a different dispensation than their own. For example, many present-day dispensationalists (not all) will read about the miracles in the New Testament and have no thought as to whether those things could happen today. Because they see the disciples of Jesus as living in a distinctly different time period than our Church Age, they see no reason why we should expect God to act that way now.

The dispensational worldview also tends to see history as stagnant within any one dispensation. For example, dispensationalists see the Church during the present Age of Grace as unchanging. They believe Christians must endeavor to expand the Church in size through missionary endeavors; however, they also must keep Her on the same course which She has been traveling for the last 2,000 years. Dispensationalists see themselves as the defenders of the faith, standing against an onslaught of the devil and a big evil world. They must continue this fight until Jesus returns, that is, until the next dispensation.

Bringing the Future into Focus

The dispensational way of thinking is a relatively recent development in Church history. This worldview became especially strong after the *Scofield Reference Bible* was published in 1909. It gave a commentary along with the Scriptures showing the dealings of God divided into distinct time periods. Many influential American leaders during the early 1900's embraced this view of the Bible and history, promoting it widely.

Today, dispensational Christians tend to dominate Christian radio and television programs. Christians who never have had dispensational thinking explained to them, nor ever even heard of the word, *dispensation*, have sat under the teachings of leaders who think dispensationally. The truth is that all Christian denominations have been influenced to some extent by the dispensational worldview.

Unfortunately, many Christians never have been exposed to other worldviews. They sit quietly listening to their favorite preacher and they think about the topics being addressed. However, they rarely, if ever, question the deeper foundational worldview underlying the preacher's message and thought processes. Because they never have been presented with any other worldview, they have nothing with which they can compare.

The Restorational Worldview

Evangelical Christians who hold to the *restorational worldview* believe that God is going to restore the present Church to the conditions She experienced in the New Testament.

Their image of the early Church is exalted. Restorationalists see the apostles working miracles as thousands of souls are saved. The first believers moved in unity and power. Restorationalists picture the early Church in an ideal state with believers loving each other so much that they were selling their possessions and holding things in common.

Restorational Christians look at the years following the First Century as a time during which the Church began declining from Her original glory and power. They envision religious leaders gradually developing a governmental hierarchy and placing one man-made tradition after another upon the Christian people. As Christianity became weighted down with carnal rules and ritualistic practices, they conclude that the Church lost Her original innocence, glory, and power.

The restorational Christian points to the Dark Ages (400 to 1450 AD) as the lowest point in history, the time during which the established Church was farthest removed from what God intended for the Body of Christ.

However, in the mind of the restorational Christian there is a hope and positive side for God's people. They believe that after the Dark Ages, beginning about 1450 AD, God began restoring the Church back to Her original glory, purity, and power. They do not see this restorational process happening quickly, but slowly, as God sends one leader after another proclaiming biblical truths and bringing the Church along one step at a time. This restorational process is continuing today, they say, and before the end of the world the Church will be restored completely to Her status on Pentecost Day.

Notice how this view of the Church differs from dispensational thinking. The dispensationalist sees the Church relatively stagnant. It actively may change in size; however, the message and condition of the Church remains constant until the next intervention of God and the end of this present dispensation. Restorationalists envision God more active and the Church advancing to a condition of glory and a position of victory.

When restorational Christians study the Old Testament, they see it through "restorational eyes"; they see the events recorded in the Old Testament as "foreshadowings" of what God is doing in the Church throughout time. For example, the Jews moving into the Promised Land is seen as a picture of how Christians today can and will move into the promises God has for us. The temple built in the time of Solomon is seen as a picture of the temple which God is now building in the Church—we are that temple of God. As the Old Testament is viewed as a foreshadowing of

God's New Testament plan, principles are taken from it and applied to the modern Church and the ongoing Christian life.

The Advancement of Time in the Mind of the Restorational Christian

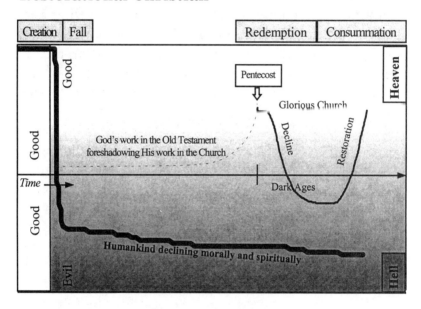

Restorational teaching has been growing in recent years. Although there have been leaders with related views spotting the last 200 years of Church history (i.e., Aimee Semple McPherson, the founder of the Four Square denomination during the 1920's), it became more visible in America during the *Latter Rain Movement* beginning in 1948. At that time a revival in Canada attracted tens of thousands of Evangelical Christians offering them a fresh manifestation of the Holy Spirit and some revelatory teachings, including the belief that God would raise His Church to glory and power before Jesus returned to the Earth. Many leaders eagerly embraced this hopeful message and began incorporating it into their books and preaching.

Today there are fewer restorationalists than dispensationalists; however, more and more dispensationalists are changing their views and moving into the restorational camp. Let me show you why.

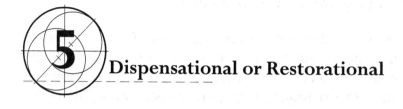

Dispensational or Restorational

Having ministered in hundreds of churches, I would much rather teach Christians who have a restorational worldview than those who have a dispensational outlook. As we mentioned earlier, many dispensational Christians conveniently excuse themselves from expecting God to work in ways that He did in a different time period. In contrast, restorational Christians have an expectancy that God will do in the Church today anything which He did in the New Testament times, and they expect supernatural manifestations to increase as we approach the end of times. I like that.

Furthermore, those with a dispensational outlook see the Church Age as relatively stagnant, and therefore, a Christian's job primarily is to defend the truths already revealed. Faithful church members eagerly support and give a staunch "Amen!" to the preacher who is repeating the beliefs they feel responsible to defend.

A restorational group of Christians enjoys hearing affirmations of their faith, but they also have their ears tuned to *what God is restoring next.* They see the Church moving in a positive direction. As the children of Israel followed the pillar of fire across the wilderness, so the restorational Christian believes the Church is following the Holy Spirit into the fulfillment of God's promises and blessings. Therefore, they want to learn what God is restoring to the Church next and lay hold of a hope for positive advancement.

Because of these differing worldviews, the dispensational Christian and the restorational Christian have much different receptivities to messages which they hear.

The dispensational group of believers has strong resistance to learning truths they have not heard before. Of course, they may be doing their best to incorporate new methods of sharing the Gospel, and they actively may be looking for effective ways to minister to the society around them—indeed, they typically excel in these areas. However, their worldview is restrictive in the sense that it leads them to be very cautious. Any new direction being presented may be viewed as the enemy of "the faith once delivered to their forefathers."

In addition, dispensationalism allows adherents to "compartmentalize" people groups more distinctly than other worldviews. In particular, in the Old Testament, they see God dealing primarily with the Jewish people, hence, it is natural to see the Jews as very distinct from other nations. So also in the present dispensation the Church is seen as very separate from the rest of the world, with the Church and the world at two ends of the spectrum. With this compartmentalized way of viewing time and people groups, there is a greater tendency to see one group as "in God's favor" while another is not—a way of thinking which we later will see as having significant implications.

As I minister to dispensational Christians I find them to be very defensive and, at times, opposing

Scriptural truths that are new to them. In contrast, Christians with a restorational worldview are much more open and have great hope for the future of the Church.

This being true, I still want you to keep in mind that many truths of the Christian faith should be rigorously defended, as our dispensational brothers and sisters in Christ do so well. When I compare these different worldviews, I am pointing out advantages of one over the other. Each has positive points; however, I am attempting to develop the most biblically-accurate perspective, which I believe is the progressive worldview.

6 The Progressive Worldview

The *progressive worldview* recognizes that from before the foundations of the world God has had a plan which He is working out through the ages. He has an end goal in mind to sum up all things in Jesus. Everything God has done since Creation is with a view to that goal, and He is working out His plan in a progressive fashion.

The apostle Paul gives us a glimpse of this view when he wrote about the workings of God throughout time:

> *He made known to us the mystery of His will, according to His kind intention which He purposed in Him with a view to an administration suitable to the fullness of the times, that is, the summing up of all things in Christ, things in the heavens and things upon the earth....who works all things after the counsel of His will.*
> (Eph. 1:9-11)

God has a plan with an end goal in mind. Throughout this book we will be explaining what that plan is and what God is doing in the Church and in the world according to that plan.

In order to embrace the progressive worldview, you must focus on the work of God rather than the

Fall and corruption of humanity. Christians with a progressive worldview recognize humanity's sin, however, they focus on God confidently working out His plan through the ages in spite of humanity's failures.

The progressive Christian sees all of God's actions recorded in the Bible as steps toward His ultimate goal, which is to sum up all things in Jesus. At Creation, God had the end goal in mind. When Adam and Eve sinned, He took actions to continue directing things toward that same goal. When God spoke to Abraham and called his descendants to be His people, this was part of His overall plan. We see the hand of God during the Jewish captivity in Egypt, through their wanderings in the wilderness, and their eventual inhabiting of the Promised Land. Similarly, God was working out His plan guiding the family lineage of David and establishing the Jews as a nation. Just as significant and interwoven are all the words that the prophets spoke throughout the Old Testament concerning the Jewish people and the coming Kingdom.

In sequence, yet in the same picture, place John the Baptist stepping onto the scene, then our Lord Jesus living, dying, resurrecting, and then sitting down at the right hand of the Father.

Now envision the early Church proclaiming the Gospel and advancing throughout the last 2,000 years. See Her as heading toward a glorious day of unity, holiness, and power. Do not picture any major decline of glory during the last 2,000 years (we will see why later), but rather see a continual progression upward according to God's plan.

Envision one picture, start to finish, of God's gradual, progressive, step-by-step, unfolding plan culminating in the ultimate and total rule of Jesus Christ.

The Advancement of Time in the Mind of the Progressive Christian

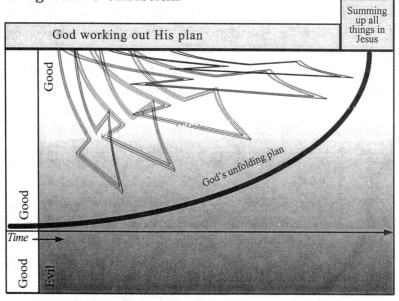

The diagram above offers a very simplified and generalized picture of the progressive worldview. In reality, the progression of God's plan should not be seen as smoothly unfolding but rather filled with "bumps on the road." Also, the diagram above is not meant to imply that everything in this world is getting better and better. Not all of humanity responds to the ongoing work of God. Many people have and will continue to rebel, attempting to move in the opposite direction of God's will. The smooth ascending line in our diagram is meant to portray God confidently working out His plan in the midst of the world. We will see this and numerous other points of the progressive worldview as we continue to fill in the details throughout the remaining portion of this book.

I will be comparing the progressive worldview with the dispensational and restorational worldviews, emphasizing the advantages of the progressive. I do not want to offend any of my brothers or sisters in Christ who hold more tightly to dispensational or restorational perspectives. For much of my Christian life, I was trained to think and teach from both of those positions. Now, I simply want to explain to my friends why I have come to embrace the progressive view as more beneficial, enlightening, and biblically accurate.

In order to explain, I have been and will continue to give simplified definitions and descriptions of the three views. I do not mean to over-simplify nor over-generalize. I use clear-cut terminology because it is necessary to open people's eyes to see how they themselves may be thinking and living—often without realizing it.

There are dispensational, restorational, and progressive Christians who cross over into the other ways of thinking or combine them when talking about specific areas of discussion. Therefore, we should not categorize someone as "completely dispensational" or "completely restorational."

In fact, I do not want to be thought of as completely progressive. As I mentioned, it would be wrong to think of God's plan moving forward in time, proceeding in a perfectly smooth uphill fashion. Certainly there have been catastrophic setbacks in history and definite points in time when huge steps forward were taken. For example, the destruction in Noah's day can be seen as a major setback. On the other hand, the resurrection of Jesus must be seen as a triumphal moment which is more than a gradual step ahead. Indeed, at the moments identified as transitional points by the dispensationalists, things were not gradual but rather dramatic.

Recognizing this, I will be talking about *tendencies* in Christians' thinking. Some Christians gravitate toward dispensational thinking, others restorational, and others progressive. I hope I can convince you to have a stronger tendency to be more progressive in your thinking.

The Original Blessing

Christians who hold to any one of the three world-views believe the Bible to be inspired by God; however, they have different ways of interpreting the Bible.

If you were to visit three churches and the associated ministers were teaching on the same Bible verse, you would learn that each minister explains that verse through his own worldview. Although all three ministers believe the Bible, they will develop very different teachings and arrive at very different conclusions.

This is especially evident with Bible passages where God intervened in the affairs of humankind. For example, after God created the world, He blessed Adam and Eve:

> *And God blessed them; and God said to them, "Be fruitful and multiply, fill the earth, and subdue it...."* (Gen. 1:28)

A dispensational teacher first would place this verse in a time frame, that is, in the dispensation which he already has established in his mind. He will explain that it was God's original intention for people to be fruitful and successful on the Earth. However, because Adam and Eve sinned, humankind never will fulfill God's original plan, and hence, that dispensation quickly ended. Before finishing his message, he most likely will redirect the listeners' attention to the present dispensation (the Church Age) and discuss how God is offering grace and redemption in our time.

A restorational minister will explain Genesis 1:28 through "restorational eyes." In other words, he will see Pentecost as the pinnacle of history and express great hope for the restoration of the Church to the glory She experienced on Pentecost Day.

The restorational preacher will read Genesis 1:28, and after explaining the historical context, he will say that Adam and Eve later sinned and, therefore, failed at the great commission which God gave to humankind to be fruitful and multiply. However, he then will offer hope. Through the use of an allegory, he will compare Adam and Eve with Jesus and the Church. Adam failed, but now there is a New Adam, that is, Jesus Christ. Indeed, Jesus and the Church are the Groom and Bride Who actually will become fruitful, multiply, and fulfill God's first commission to humankind.

Now, consider how a minister with a progressive worldview would teach from the same Bible passage. He, too, believes the Bible to be the Word of God; however, he sees every act of God as progressively building and leading to the fulfillment of God's ultimate plan.

When the progressive minister preaches from Genesis 1:28, he first notes that these Words of God were spoken over Adam and Eve as a *blessing*. To see this, read that verse again.

The Original Blessing

And God blessed them; and God said to them, "Be fruitful and multiply, fill the earth, and subdue it...." (Gen. 1:28)

God spoke the same words, "be fruitful and multiply," over the fish and birds (Gen. 1:22). Hence, we should not think of these words as a commission or a command that animals or people are being ordered to fulfill. Both times we are told that this is how God "blessed" them. It is more accurate to think of this as *God's original blessing*, rather than His first commission.

This is important because a blessing is a release of God's power and favor. The Hebrew word from which "blessed" has been translated shares the same root as the Hebrew word for "create." Whenever God speaks, His Words produce what they are sent out to produce. He made this clear when He spoke through Isaiah saying:

"So shall My word be which goes out
from My mouth;
It shall not return to Me empty,
Without accomplishing what I
desire,
And without succeeding in the
matter for which I send it."
(Is. 55:11)

Just as God's Words at Creation brought things into existence, so also God's Words over Adam and Eve released a force to produce exactly what He said.

33

Bringing the Future into Focus

Therefore, God's Words—His original blessing— still act upon Adam and Eve's descendants, that is, all of humankind today. Yes, there is a force which originated with God, motivating and even pushing people to be fruitful, multiply, fill, subdue, and have dominion over the Earth. (When I use these words *subdue* and *dominion* here and in the rest of this book, I do not mean to imply the negative connotation of abuse of the natural environment, but rather to use wisely, care for, and steward the Earth.)

The Progressive Worldview Showing God's Original Blessing

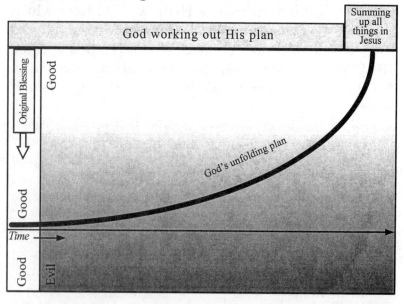

What does God's original blessing mean for us today? There is a force pushing humankind to advance. It is like a wave emanating from the mouth of

34

God in the distant past. At the forefront of that wave today are people with new ideas, medical break-throughs, management techniques, new inventions, engineering solutions, and every other step of progress helping humankind to fill, use wisely, and manage the Earth.*

Adam and Eve sinned, but they did not frustrate the plan of God. The progressive teacher sees God taking one step when He created this world and put things in motion, then another step when He blessed humankind. Nothing can stop the power of God's original blessing. Humankind is and will continue multiplying, filling, and subduing the Earth.

Now think of all three worldviews and how pro-foundly they change how a certain minister or any Christian understands the same Bible verse. Because the dispensational teacher makes everything fit into his preset time frames, he sees a beginning and an end to God's plan for Adam and Eve to fill and subdue the Earth. The restorational minister also sees a beginning and an end to that plan, but then he uses an analogy to talk about God's new plan in Jesus and the Church. The progressive Christian sees that no part of God's plan ever fails, and everything He does is progressively building toward His preordained goal.

Notice also *who* is impacted by God's Words in Genesis 1:28. The dispensational view teaches that Adam and Eve failed, and hence, God's Words no longer have direct significance for our daily lives. The

---

* For more teaching on God's original blessing, read *The Nature of Creation*, Vol. 6 in the Spiritual Realities series. Information on how to obtain this book is in the Appendix.

restorational view similarly sees Adam and Eve's failure, but through an analogy teaches that the Church will fill and subdue all with Jesus. The progressive Christian sees God's blessing still active today and acting upon all of humankind. Of course, Adam and Eve sinned, but their failure cannot subvert the plan of God. The power of His Words continue in spite of the sin of humankind. According to the progressive view, humankind—not just the Church—is moving in a direction toward successful stewardship and dominion of the Earth.

8 God's Blessing Upon Abraham

The worldview which people hold profoundly influences their interpretation of Scripture. Let me show you this with another key Bible passage.

God intervened in history when He spoke to Abram:

> *Now the Lord said to Abram,*
> *"Go forth from your country...*
> *And I will make you a great nation,*
> *And I will bless you...*
> *And in you all the families of the earth*
> *shall be blessed."*   (Gen. 12:1-3)

The dispensational minister declares that a new dispensation began through God's dealings with Abraham. God initiated a covenant with Abraham, and Abraham's descendants became a special people called to Himself. As a consequence, the Jews had favor with God for the dispensation to follow.

If the dispensational minister goes on to discuss the end of that dispensation, he will explain that the Jewish people repeatedly rebelled against God and eventually rejected Jesus as the Messiah. Hence, they have been set aside by God and their dispensation of favor is over.*

---

* Most dispensational teachers believe that the Jews will get one more dispensation of God's favor after the present Church Age.

Bringing the Future into Focus

If we listen to a restorational minister teach from the same verses (Gen. 12:1-3), we also will hear him say that God called the Jewish people to Himself, but they rebelled, rejected the Messiah, and lost favor in God's eyes. However, the restorational minister loves to develop analogies comparing God's Old Testament people to His New Testament people. As God blessed Abraham and his descendants, so also He blessed Jesus Christ and those who have been reborn through Him.

Countless other analogies can be drawn between God's dealings with the Jews and His dealings with Christians. Some favorite analogies of restorational teachers are:

- As the Jews wandered through the wilderness until they made it into the Promised Land and so the Church will work through the trials and obstacles of life until She walks into the full promises of God.
- Just as there was a temple in the Old Testament, so also there is a temple now, which is us, His people.
- As God built the tabernacle for the Jews, so also He is building us to be a tabernacle where He will come and dwell.

These and other analogies can be used to teach the fundamental doctrine of restorationalism: that God is restoring the Church and raising Her up to maturity.

Of course, there are wonderful truths in these dispensational and restorational teachings; however, the progressive view has a more complete perspective to offer. If a minister were to teach on Genesis 12:1-3 from the progressive view, he would explain that God intervened in history during the life of Abraham and called a people to Himself. However, the progressive minister would emphasize different aspects of God's words to Abraham.

First, it was a blessing, not a covenant. Later in Genesis we can read of several times when God appeared to Abraham and entered into covenant with him (i.e., Gen. 15:12-18). However, in Genesis 12:1-3 we read about God's *blessing* upon Abraham. As we discussed earlier, each of God's blessings releases a positive force which continues until all is fulfilled.

Second, this blessing is for Abraham's natural and spiritual descendants. He had two natural sons, Isaac (through his wife Sarah) and Ishmael (through Sarah's maidservant). Isaac became the father of the Jewish people and Ishmael is the father of today's Arab people. Isaac was the child of promise, and hence, his descendants received the full blessings of God which were given to Abraham. Ishmael also received a blessing to become a great nation (Gen. 16:10-11), but his blessing is less significant and of a more legalistic, rather than a grace-filled, nature (Gal. 4:21-30).

In the New Testament we learn that Abraham also has spiritual descendants, that is, those who have faith in Abraham's Seed—Jesus Christ(Gal. 3:6-14). Therefore, Gentiles who believe in Jesus are grafted into the blessings of Abraham (Rom. 11:17-20).

Even though these blessings come upon the Jews, the Christian Gentiles, and in a limited way the

Arabs, they are meant to bless the whole Earth. God told Abraham, "...*in you all the families of the earth shall be blessed*" (Gen. 12:3). Notice how this blessing reaches far beyond the Jewish and Christian people, even to *all* the families of the whole Earth.

Picture this: several thousand years ago, God blessed Abraham. Today we can see evidence of this. In nations where Christianity (especially Protestant Christianity) and Judaism are the dominant religions, society experiences greater blessings. Generally speaking, health is better, prosperity is greater, and people have more freedom. Even the Arabs are a great people of tremendous strength. In contrast, wherever religions such as Hinduism, Buddhism, Confucianism, witchcraft, and ancestral worship are dominant, people typically live in much worse and limiting conditions. It is a fact that wherever Abraham's natural and spiritual descendants are in the Earth, the people there are more blessed.

Furthermore, the whole Earth has benefited from the advancements in education, literature, health, government, technology, etc., which have come through the spiritual and natural descendants of Abraham.*

In the overall picture of passing time, the progressive Christian sees God's intervention in Abraham's life as one more step in the unfolding plan of God.

---

* Most people in the Western world are unaware of the tremendous contributions which Arab people have made to the advancement of society. Historians recognize that during the Middle Ages the Arab culture was more developed educationally, philosophically, and politically than the non-Arab European world.

The Progressive Worldview Adding God's Blessings Upon Abraham

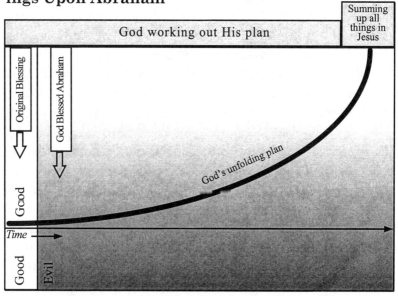

Consider how differently various Christian groups view Genesis 12:1-3. The dispensationalist tends to limit God's Words as applicable to the Jewish people for a time past. The restorationalists also see God's Words applying to a people of the past, but they use an analogy to teach about greater things available for the Church through Jesus Christ. The progressive Christians agree that there are greater blessings through Jesus, yet they also say that God's blessing upon Abraham is still active and that blessing has consequences for all of humankind today.

Further, the progressive Christian sees that the same Words spoken to Abraham apply to our lives. You and I can say, "Through us God will bless the whole Earth."

Bringing the Future into Focus

Dispensational Christians may stretch themselves in mental assent to this truth; however, they cannot fully embrace it. They have too strong of a mindset about God's dealings with Abraham as belonging to another people and another time period.

Christians with a restorational worldview may also say that the blessings of Abraham have come upon them; however, it is in an analogous fashion. If they say they are blessed as Abraham was blessed, they mean that they have blessings analogous to the blessings of Abraham. They would prefer to say that they have blessings better than the blessings of Abraham.

It is true that Christians have greater blessings; however, the progressive Christians also understand that the *very blessings* which God spoke to Abraham are still active today. Those very Words are true for our lives.

Embrace the Old Testament

Dispensational, restorational, and progressive Christians all will say that the whole Bible has meaning for us today; however, each group interprets the Bible through their own worldview. As a consequence, they actually embrace some parts of the Bible and unknowingly distance themselves from other passages.

Dispensational Christians break the Old Testament into several distinct dispensations separate from the present Church Age. This leaves many truths and words of the Old Testament not directly applicable to our lives today. As we saw earlier, they identify the sin of Adam and Eve as the end of the first dispensation, and, therefore, the Words of God to fill and subdue the Earth have little meaning for them. As we also discussed, dispensational Christians see little meaning for themselves in the blessing God gave to Abraham. Instead, they see it as God's covenant meant for the Jewish people. There are many other examples I could give here and some I will mention later; however, at this point I hope you can see how dispensational thinking leads one to compartmentalize the events, activities, and promises recorded in the Bible to specific times and people groups. Of course, there are some occasions when this is helpful, yet other times when it is very limiting.

Bringing the Future into Focus

Dispensational Christians think of the dispensations preceding the New Testament as God's attempts to reach out to humanity, yet all those attempts fade in glory in comparison with His reaching through Jesus. There is truth to that perspective; however, it degrades God's actions throughout the Old Testament. An inescapable implication of exalting the Church Age as God's best attempt is the lowering of preceding dispensations as God's lesser attempts. Although dispensationalists would defend their position and say that I am being too critical in making this judgment, I will say that, *through the eyes of a Christian with a progressive worldview*, it appears that dispensationalists think of God's actions recorded in the Old Testament as His inferior or even failed plans.

Restorational Christians see the activities of God in the Old Testament not as failures but as *foreshadowings* of God's true plans. As I explained, they see God's Words to Adam and Eve as the foreshadowing of what God intends to do through Jesus and the Church. They view the covenant made with Abraham as a foreshadowing of the better covenant which God has made through Jesus with Christians. Other examples can be added, but I trust you can already see the eyes through which the restorational Christian tends to view the Old Testament.

In the mind of the dispensational and restorational Christian, there is a clear demarcation which causes them to see the Old Testament through distant and clouded eyes. Both have consciously and subconsciously erected a wall between the Old and New Testaments which diminishes the value and relevance of the Old Testament for us today.

In contrast, progressive Christians see the Bible as one book. Everything God accomplished in Old Testament times is a foundation (not a failed plan, nor merely a foreshadowing) of their own faith today. God's original blessing upon Adam and Eve is still moving society ahead. God's Words to Abraham continue to bring prosperity and solutions to problems in the world around us. These and every act of God recorded in the Old Testament are steps toward the end goal which God has in mind for this world.

Christians holding the three worldviews all say that they believe the Old Testamont, but in reality, only the progressive Christians embrace it equally with the New Testament. They see the Bible as one book.

10 The Promise of the Kingdom

My goal is to develop a picture of the overall plan of God through the ages. After developing that picture, we will be able to see clearly where God is taking the Church and the whole world. There are hundreds of passages we could examine to help us form that picture; however, it is the *perspective of the progressive worldview* which enables you to see the unfolding plan of God. Once you have grasped that perspective, you will be able to see the future more clearly.

I will focus on one more key Bible passage to make sure you have grasped the difference between the perspectives offered by the dispensational, restorational, and progressive worldviews.

Consider when God intervened and spoke to King David, making a covenant to establish a kingdom:

> *...I will set up one of your descendants after you, who shall be of your sons; and I will establish his kingdom. He shall build for Me a house, and I will establish his throne forever....I will settle him in My house and in My kingdom forever, and his throne shall be established forever.* (I Chron. 17:11-14)

A dispensationalist will explain the historical event in a specific time period—in that dispensation.

He will explain that God's promise was fulfilled as Solomon, the son of David, was raised to sit on the throne over a natural kingdom ruling over the Jewish people. He also might talk about the promise for a future kingdom and that another descendant of David, that is, Jesus, will rule over a spiritual kingdom. However, the dispensational minister sees the natural kingdom of the Jews as separate and belonging to a different dispensation than the spiritual kingdom over which Jesus Christ will reign. Seeing two different kingdoms, the dispensationalist will infer that the natural kingdom failed* and the spiritual kingdom is a success.

Similarly, the restorationalist preacher sees two separate kingdoms, but he enjoys drawing analogies between them. He will infer that the natural kingdom was a success to some extent, but inferior to and a foreshadowing of the true kingdom.

In contrast, the progressive teacher sees only one successful Kingdom. In preaching from I Chronicles 17:11-14, they may discuss the historical event when God spoke to King David. They also may draw analogies as the restorationalist teacher does. However, the main distinction in their view is that the Kingdom that was promised to the Jews in the Old Testament is the *same Kingdom* of which Christians are a part today. Jesus Christ is sitting "on the throne of David" (Is. 9:6-7).

---

* Most dispensationalists believe that the natural kingdom of the Jews will be re-established and successfully set up in the future on the Earth during the Millennium.

That same Kingdom was extended (progressed) beyond the Promised Land when Jesus was exalted to the right hand of God. Citizenship in that Kingdom has been expanded to include all who put their faith in King Jesus, not just Jewish people. Those who do not put their faith in this King will be rejected from the Kingdom, whether Jews or Gentiles. However, according to the progressive Christian, the Kingdom over which Jesus now reigns has been progressively advancing since it was promised to King David.

The Progressive Worldview Adding God's Promise to David Concerning the Kingdom

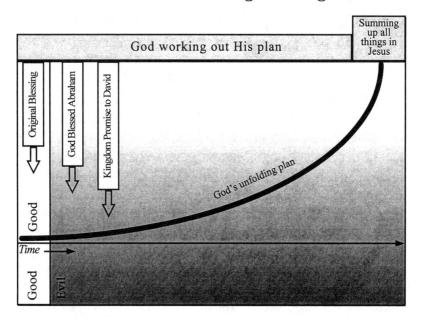

To clarify how the Kingdom promised in the Old Testament is the same Kingdom over which Jesus now reigns, examine the parable which Jesus told in Matthew 21:33-40. Jesus told of a landowner who left his vineyard in the care of vinegrowers while he went away on a journey. About harvest time, the landowner sent slaves to receive his portion of the harvest, but the vinegrowers beat and killed the slaves. Then the landowner sent his son to receive the harvest, but he, too, was killed by the vinegrowers. Jesus told this parable in the presence of the chief priests and Pharisees, revealing that they were as the vinegrowers, rejecting the son of the landowner (Matt. 21:33-45). Then Jesus warned them saying:

> *"Therefore I say to you, the kingdom of God will be taken away from you, and be given to a nation producing the fruit of it."* (Matt. 21:43)

The Kingdom of God was taken out of the hands of the Jewish religious leaders and made available to those who produce appropriate fruit.

Notice that I am not teaching "Replacement Theology," that is, the doctrine which says Christians have replaced the Jews in respect to receiving the promises of God. In a later chapter, I will discuss the covenant which God has with the Jews and what their future will be. Here, I simply am pointing out that the Kingdom which was promised to the Jews is the same Kingdom over which Jesus now reigns. The religious leaders rejected the King of that Kingdom. However, the one Kingdom which once was promised to the Jews has progressed and is now available to Jews and Gentiles who receive King Jesus.

11 Restorational Idealism

I hope it is obvious how the dispensational world-view can be defensive and limiting. Many dispensationalists deny the function or place for God currently to work through the miraculous, as He has in other times. Dispensationalism distances Christians from the Old Testament. It also offers no hope for the Church to rise in glory, power, and maturity before the return of Christ.

While recognizing the importance of defending the basic truths of Christianity, let us set aside for a moment the dispensational view and turn our attention to the restorational view to identify a major misconception upon which it is based.

Christians with a restorational worldview picture the Church being restored to Her status on the Day of Pentecost, as described in the book of Acts. However, restorational Christians have an idealistic view of the early Church. They think that we would be better off going back to the First-Century form of Christianity. But this is a serious mistake because it was not as grand as restorational Christians tend to believe.

The First-Century believers were struggling with issues that most Christians today have long since settled. For example, the Apostle Paul had to write to the Romans, the Ephesians, and the Galatians trying to convince them that salvation comes by grace through faith. He wrote to the Corinthian believers to convince them, among other things, that there will be a resurrection of the dead (I Cor. 15). The Apostle John wrote to fight against the beliefs of Gnosticism which taught that Jesus was not human, but only a spirit.

The early Church did not have the complete New Testament. During the First and Second Centuries there were many letters circulating among the early believers, all teaching various doctrines and practices claiming to be the teachings of Jesus. The confusion that resulted from not having one standard for truth was no small matter. Add to this the fact that they had no means of mass communication, such as radio, television, or even printing presses. Today we are so far removed from that time period we cannot realize fully how difficult it actually was. Several generations were without the full New Testament—think about if that time period were moved to the last 200 years preceding your lifetime. You can see that it was a major problem.

The greatest arguments among Christians during the First Century concerned Gentiles becoming Christians. While Paul was preaching freely and openly to the Gentiles, Peter did it secretly (Gal. 2:11-14). Other Christian leaders were divided over the issue, and it was not until about 15 years after Pentecost (as recorded in Acts 15) that the leaders even got together to decide whether Gentiles should be allowed in the Christian congregations without keeping all of the Jewish Laws. Please consider this seriously. If you had been a Gentile during the early Church, how would you have survived, received teaching, or matured in that environment? It was not easy.

Furthermore, the teachings about Jesus as both man and God were not clarified until the Fourth through Sixth Centuries. The average Christian today has a much better understanding of this than the First-Century believers.

In idealizing the early Church, restorational Christians like to point out that 3,000 souls were saved on Pentecost Day. However, that is a very small number compared with people being saved today. It is fairly common now for 3,000 people to receive Jesus in one modern evangelistic crusade. If we look at the whole worldwide picture, we see 3,000 souls being added to the Church about every 25 minutes of every day. In comparison, the revival on Pentecost Day was small and only in one location.

Why is this so important? Because I am challenging the restorational view right at its foundation. They idealistically view the New Testament Church and wrongly want us to be restored to that condition. That would be foolish. The Church is much better off today than it was back then.

There is one verse in the Bible used by restorational Christians more than any other to support their worldview. It is Acts 3:20-21, where we are told:

> *...and that He may send Jesus, the Christ appointed for you, whom heaven must receive until the period of restoration of all things about which God spoke by the mouth of His holy prophets from ancient time.*

Bringing the Future into Focus

Restorational Christians like to quote these verses and speak about the "period of restoration" as if it will precede the return of Jesus and cause the Church to return to the conditions She experienced on Pentecost Day.

That is a misinterpretation. Yes, there will be a period of restoration; however, these verses are speaking of a much greater and far-reaching restoration than what the restorational Christian has in mind. Please read Acts 3:20-21 carefully. What does it say will happen? This is a promise, not that the endtime Church will be restored to New Testament Christianity, but rather that everything God has spoken through each and every one of "His holy prophets from ancient time" will be fulfilled.

That is a major distinction and a key point: Acts 3:20-21 points us *not* back to New Testament Christianity, but to the fulfillment of *all* God has promised. Recognizing this, we must say that this passage does not support the restorational view, but rather the progressive view.

Furthermore, we need to understand that the Church will grow into a "mature man," (Eph. 4:12-13), not be restored to what She experienced as a newborn infant.

Rethinking Church History

In addition to idealistic views of the First-Century Church, restorational Christians foster a distorted perception of the Church of the Fourth to Sixteenth Centuries (300-1500 AD). They envision the Church straying from the original purity, holiness, and power of New-Testament Christianity during that time. While there is some truth to this, the negative aspects are exaggerated to the exclusion of the positive.

One point in history viewed by restorationalists as a major turning point toward the decline of Christianity is the year 313 AD, when the Roman Emperor Constantine began making Christianity the privileged religion of the Empire. Preceding this date, Christians were persecuted severely, which demanded great commitment to endure. In the few years that followed 313 AD, hundreds of thousands of people claimed new allegiance to the Christian faith. In the eyes of restorational Christians today, that is interpreted as the time when Christianity became socially acceptable and, therefore, lukewarm and impotent.

The year 313 AD also is known as the point when the state and religion joined arms. The Roman Empire embraced Christianity, and, as a result, tremendous authority was granted to the religious leaders in Rome. Gradually, the Roman Catholic Church emerged on the forefront of the western Christian world, and the forms of worship and doctrinal beliefs that it espoused became the most accepted throughout Europe. A hierarchy of Church government began to form, and one ritual after another was added to the Church liturgy and daily practice. Many Church leaders are known to have committed sexual sins. The established Church began accepting certain doctrines that Protestants today label as unbiblical, such as the veneration of Mary, exaltation of the pope, existence of purgatory, and use of indulgences. At the same time certain beliefs, especially those associated with Greek thought, were synthesized into the Church resulting in some pagan concepts being embraced by the mainstream of Christianity.

Restorational Christians have a tendency to focus on these negative points of history to reinforce their view of the Church declining in glory after the Third Century. In referring to the period from 400 to 1450 AD, restorationalists like to use the label "Dark Ages," implying that the world was slipping into deeper and deeper darkness.

Restorational Christians see the period after the Dark Ages as the "period of restoration" where God is restoring to the Church everything positive that was destroyed during the preceding 1,200 years. Since the start of the Protestant Reformation, God has been sending one leader after another, declaring Scriptural truths. God is inspiring and imparting His nature back into the Church in a step-by-step fashion. Restorationalists teach that God's restoration of the Church continues today with revelation, authority, holiness, and power increasing.

The Restorational Worldview Showing Their Perspective of Church History

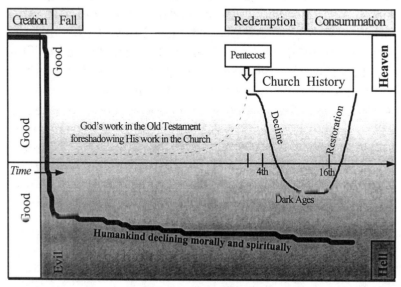

Many of my readers already have been exposed to such a view of Church history. Admittedly, there are many truths and historical facts that are incorporated into books and teachings which promote this view. Indeed, if we focus only on certain problems in the Church, we can develop a declining view of the early Church, followed by a period of restoration. However, there are several reasons why I cannot embrace the restorational view of Church history.

Consider the year 313, the time that restorational Christians call the greatest turning point toward the decline of Christianity. The Roman Emperor Constantine made Christianity the accepted religion of the empire. Was this positive or negative? It is true that there were many, perhaps multitudes, who claimed to be Christians without making true commitments. However, to see that transition only in a negative light is to miss the major outcome—the exploding growth of Christianity. Previous to that date, Christians primarily met in secret, but now the Gospel was being preached openly. History tells us that the overwhelming majority of the Roman Empire claimed to be Christian by the end of the Fifth Century.*

The Kingdom of God rapidly advanced, then and in the years to follow. During the Fifth Century, Patrick preached in Ireland, and the vast majority of people were converted from paganism to Christianity. The Celtic Church became very evangelistic during the Sixth Century, and Columba successfully led missionaries who overwhelmingly replaced pagan priests and the druids throughout Scotland. During the same time, the Roman Catholic Church was instrumental in leading thousands of people in England into a belief in Jesus Christ. In the Eighth Century, Boniface led in the successful evangelization of Germany. One of the most rapid growth periods for Christianity was between 950 and 1050 AD. Denmark, Norway, Sweden, Iceland, and Greenland responded to the Gospel. The Eastern Orthodox Church made great inroads into what is now called Russia. Large percentages of the Czechs and Poles became Christian. Many Arabs who previously were Muslim also were converted, while at the same time the Nestorian Christians made great advances into Asia, being especially successful establishing churches in China and India. The Roman

---

* Kenneth Scott Lattourette, *A History of Christianity*, Vol. I, (New York: Harper and Row, 1975) 97.

Catholic Church also made great advances in these areas.

We could look critically at that expansion of Christianity and say that the Gospel they were preaching was not exactly like Evangelical Protestants preach today, but realize that people were hearing about Jesus Christ for the first time. The masses of people previously were lost in darkness, worshipping nature, false gods, the dead, or humans who claimed to be gods. Whether or not we agree with everything that was preached, we must admit that the Fourth to Sixteenth Centuries were times of incredible, triumphant expansion for Christianity. When viewed from the perspective of the Kingdom of God growing, Christianity was *very successful*.

Restorational Christians may react and remind us that the established Church leaders began accepting certain doctrines which Protestants today label as unbiblical. I am not justifying any of those doctrines, but I believe a better way to view that time period is to recognize the failures of people in the midst of the Kingdom of God advancing.

Even the terminology, "Dark Ages," must be understood in its historical context. This label was coined by people living in the Enlightenment Period (1700's) who were labeling the generations before them as unscientific and too religious. The Dark Ages were not dark in a spiritual sense. Certainly they were difficult times, but people en masse sought God. The progressive worldview maintains that we should not think of the "Dark Ages" as a low point, but rather a time when God was confidently advancing His will in the Earth, in spite of problems.

Bringing the Future into Focus

The progressive worldview matches what our Lord said as He described how the Kingdom of God would grow throughout time. It is like a field, He said, in which a farmer planted good seed but an enemy came and also planted tares (Matt. 13:24-30); both grew up until the time of harvest. In similar fashion, there have been false ideas and doctrines sown in the Church; however, we must not lose sight of the more significant fact that true seeds are growing.

The Progressive Worldview Showing Good and Bad Growing as Seeds in a Field

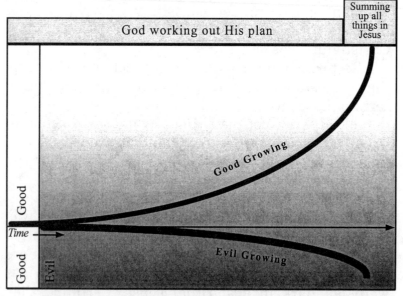

In summary, I cannot embrace the restorational view of Church history because it over-exaggerates the negative aspects while denying much good that was accomplished by the Church during the last 2,000 years.

Also, restorationalists like to think of themselves as having descended directly from the First-Century Church. Hence, they tend to remove themselves from any historical association with the form of Christianity practiced between the Fourth to Sixteenth Centuries. The idea of excluding oneself from that many years of Church history is naive. Today's Christianity has been formed by 2,000 years of leaders, relationships, evangelism, teachings, singing, books, art, debates, vocabulary development, thoughts, and battles. Good or bad, it is our history.

As one who has taught Church history at more than one Bible College, I know that scholarly studies portray the last 2,000 years in a much more progressive fashion than restorationalists would have us believe. Something which I teach my students is that if a book on Church history is less than 200 pages long, then the author has an agenda. He has chosen only a few specific events to discuss in order to form a picture which relates his own perspective. In reality, any view of Church history which even begins to offer an accurate view requires several volumes.

Finally, I must reject the restorational view of Church history because it falls short of the perspective which our Lord Jesus offered. When He gave the parable of good and bad seeds growing, He offered us the proper worldview. Both good and bad are growing in the Earth. If we embrace this progressive worldview, we can recognize and accept the positive steps made since the Protestant Reformation, along with those preceding that date.

13 Dispensational Eschatology

Now we can turn from Church history to discuss the future and endtime events—what is called *eschatology*. Although no one knows when the Second Coming of our Lord shall be, our differing worldviews tend to favor certain scenarios of what will happen between now and the final judgment.

In this chapter, I will outline the endtime events as seen by the dispensationalists. In chapter 14, we will take a quick look at the most common eschatology of the Pentecostal arm of the Church. In chapter 15, we will see the scenario envisioned by restorationalists, and then we will investigate the eschatology of progressive Christians.

As we discussed earlier, the foundation of dispensational thinking is the breaking of time into distinct periods, with God's intervention beginning and ending each dispensation. Within each dispensation God's dealings with people are seen as relatively stable. Dispensationalists believe we are presently in the dispensation of the Church, and they eagerly are looking for the next intervention of God.

Most dispensationalists believe the coming intervention will be the return of Jesus Christ to *rapture* all Christians off of the Earth. That grand event is thought to be "imminent," meaning that it could happen at anytime, without warning.

Bringing the Future into Focus

After the rapture, dispensationalists believe there will be a seven-year dispensation of tribulation,* called the "Great Tribulation" or simply the "Tribulation."

During that seven-year period, a political leader (the Antichrist) will be under the direct control of Satan and will establish an anti-Christian, anti-Jewish government over the whole world. A false religious system shall be given authority to persecute the true Church. Money shall be tightly controlled so that no one can buy or sell things unless they show allegiance to the Antichrist. It will be a time of deep spiritual darkness.

During the last half of that seven-year period, God will pour out His wrath on the world, tragic things will happen, millions will die, and destruction will be experienced across the world.

That Tribulation is thought to be a judgment period, yet it also is believed to be a time when God will turn His favor back upon the Jews. Some Gentiles will become Christians during that period, but it is primarily a time when God will vindicate the Jews, defend them against all of their enemies, and reveal to them that Jesus is the Messiah.

After the newly converted Jews and Gentiles come victoriously out of the seven-year Great Tribulation, Jesus Christ will come back to the Earth with the Christians who had earlier gone to heaven. Then

---

* Some dispensationalists believe that the rapture will take place half way through the seven-year Tribulation; however, in order to simplify our discussion we will not be explaining that view further.

Jesus will reign with His people on the Earth for 1,000 years. This 1,000-year period of peace and prosperity is considered another dispensation and called the "Millennium."

At the end of the millennial dispensation, Jesus Christ will sit on a Great White Throne and judge people. From there He will send the wicked to hell and the righteous shall be taken into heaven.

The Dispensational Worldview Showing End-time Events

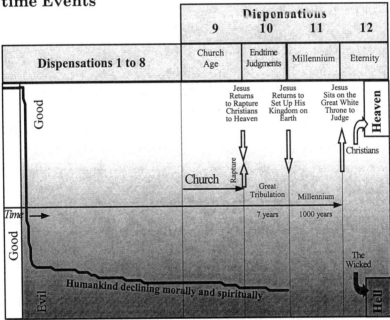

A large percentage of Evangelical Christians in America today belong to denominations and Christian groups which hold to this scenario of endtime events. Of course, many of the average church-goers sitting in the pews do not know what their leadership believes (and some don't care). This way of thinking is taught in many Evangelical Bible Colleges today (with slight variations) and is called the *Pretribulational, Premillennial view*. Pretribulational refers to Jesus returning to rapture His people off of the Earth before the Tribulation. Premillennial refers to Jesus returning before the Millennium.

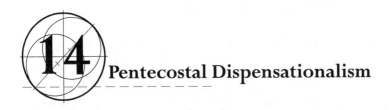

Pentecostal Dispensationalism

Most Pentecostal Christians today hold to Pre-tribulational, Premillennial eschatology. This may surprise some readers, because I have identified this endtime scenario as the sequence of events held by dispensational Christians, yet most Pentecostals today do not think of themselves as dispensational Christians. They disagree with the dispensationalists who think of the Church Age as a separate age from the time Jesus walked the Earth. They do not want to separate these two periods because they believe that the healings and miracles which happened in the New Testament should be happening in the Church today.

To understand the association of Pentecostals with dispensationalism, I need to point out that Pentecostal thinking developed out of dispensationalism. During the early 1900's, dispensational thinking became predominant among Bible-believing Christians in America. Pentecostalism grew out of that mindset.

A transition came as Pentecostals endeavored to break down the New-Testament-Age/Church-Age wall which existed in the minds of Christians. This battle was fought as Pentecostal preachers began heralding Hebrew 13:8, which says:

> *Jesus Christ is the same yesterday and today, yes and forever.*

Bringing the Future into Focus

In the early days of Pentecostalism, this verse became a rallying cry. Indeed, Pentecostal leaders were successful in breaking down the wall in the minds of their followers. People began believing that what Jesus Christ did while on Earth—miracles and healings—He will still do today through the Church. That was a victory for which many Pentecostal leaders courageously fought.

Pentecostal Christians broke down the *one* wall between the New Testament and the Church Age; however, they still are dispensationalists at the foundation of their thinking. They still have in their minds *all the other walls* which dispensationalists maintain. Most Pentecostals do not believe that what happened in the Old Testament still will happen today. For example, the blessing given to Adam and Eve has little or no significance to them. The blessings of Abraham are for another time and another people. The kingdom promised to the Jews is thought to be a different Kingdom than the one promised to Christians.

Pentecostals, for the most part, remain very much dispensational in their thinking. All they did when they trumpeted Hebrews 13:8 was lengthen, in their minds, the dispensation of the Church Age to include the time while Jesus was on the Earth.

Those who study these issues know that Christians who read the Bible through dispensational eyes, Pentecostal or non-Pentecostal, tend to embrace the Pretribulational, Premillennial scenario of endtime events.

Most Pentecostal Christians Today Hold to the Dispensational View of Endtime Events

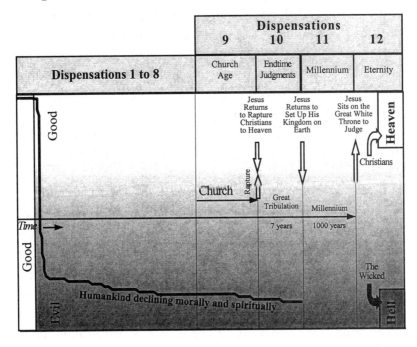

Restorational Eschatology

To see the restorational view of endtime events, remember that, above all else, they see the endtime Church being restored to Her condition in the New Testament.

Therefore, they *cannot* believe in the imminent return of Jesus Christ. They cannot believe that Jesus Christ could return at any moment, because they do not believe the Church today is measuring up to the idealistic view they have of the New-Testament Church.

As I travel to minister in churches, I find it interesting to see how confused people are on this issue. Many Christians try to hold both the dispensational belief of the imminent return of Jesus and the restorational belief that the Church first will rise in glory and power. If I stand before a typical congregation and declare to the people that Jesus Christ could return at any moment, they will nod their heads or even shout, "Amen!" Later, if I declare that God will raise His Church to glory, unity, and maturity, the same people may again say, "Amen!" In reality, the two beliefs are inconsistent. Logically, you cannot believe both.

Restorational Christians who are consistent in their own belief system teach the second viewpoint— that the Church will arise in glory before Jesus returns.

They also teach that the Church will remain here on the Earth for all or part of the Tribulation.* Instead of being raptured off of the Earth before the trials of the endtimes, they believe God will supernaturally protect His people as they go through those trials. Most restorationalists view the Tribulation as the tool of God not only to judge the world, but to test, refine, purify, and restore the Church.

According to restorationalists not all of the Church will make it. Only a "remnant" of Christians, that is, the most devout and holy, will successfully go through the Tribulation. Some restorationalists think that will be a lot of people, while others envision only a handful of Christians coming out, tested and purified. Those victorious ones are referred to as the "overcomers" or "the Bride who has made Herself ready."

Restorationalists believe that Jesus will return for His purified Bride. He will rapture the remnant off of the Earth, lifting them into heaven, while He purges the Earth of all remaining evil. Then He then come down to Earth with all of His saints to establish His Kingdom on the Earth for a 1,000 years. That 1,000-year reign is called the "Millennium."

At the end of the Millennium, the Great White Throne Judgment will occur, when everyone will stand before Jesus and be judged. The wicked will be sent to hell, and the righteous will be taken into heaven to be eternally with the Lord.

---

* Restorational teachers do not see the Tribulation as intense as Dispensationalists do. This will be discussed in chapter 19.

The Restorational Worldview Showing Endtime Events

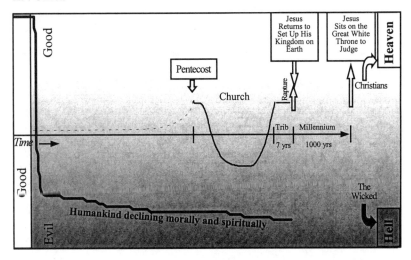

In order to simplify the diagram above, I have placed the rapture at the end of the seven-year long Tribulation; however, keep in mind that some restorationalists envision the Church being raptured before the end of the Tribulation. Other minor variations are also held by different restorational teachers, but I will limit my discussion to this commonly held restorational view.

This scenario "fits" restorationalism. It is called the Postribulational, Premillennial view. Postribulational refers to the belief that Jesus will return to rapture His people after (post) the seven-year Tribulation. Premillennial refers to the belief that Jesus will return to set up His Kingdom on Earth before the 1,000-year Millennium.

Two Forms of Premillennialism

Dispensationalism and restorationalism differ on when the rapture will take place; however, they are still both Premillennial. They both believe that after the Tribulation is completed, Jesus will return to set up His Kingdom on Earth for a 1,000-year Millennium.

Dispensational and Restorational Christians are Premillennial

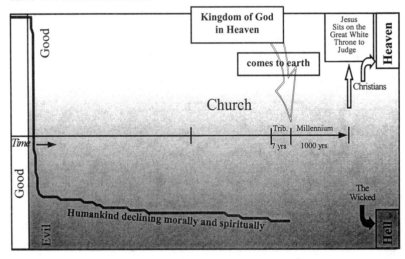

In reality, restorationalism is *basically a modified form of dispensationalism.* As we discussed earlier, dispensationalism became the dominant way of interpreting Scripture for Evangelical Christians in America during the early 1900's. Seeing its limitations, various leaders rejected the stagnant view of the Church and found new hope in restorationalism, in particular, that the Church was being raised to glory.

The vast majority of early restorationalists came out of dispensational thinking. Just as early Pentecostals had to eliminate a wall in their minds, so also the restorationalists had to abandon certain dispensational ideas. One thing they did was to trade the belief in the imminent return of Jesus for the belief in the Church arising in glory.

However, we should keep in mind that restorational thinking is rooted in dispensationalism. Just as the dispensationalists, they do not believe that God's Words to Adam and Eve still are active today. They think of God's covenant with Abraham as completely separate from God's covenant with Christians. They see the Jewish kingdom as a foreshadowing, but not the same Kingdom over which Jesus now reigns. Even though restorationalists draw many analogies between the Old Testament and the present time period, they still have definite walls erected in their minds. They still think fundamentally in terms of one distinct time period following another. They simply have moved the return of Jesus to a time after the refining of the Church.

Dispensational and restorational Christians often discuss, debate, and argue about whether there will be a rapture before or after the Tribulation. Usually, they do not realize that the scenario of endtime events cannot be separated from a Christian's entire view of history and the Bible. It is not a matter of finding some Scripture verse and then saying that it teaches

Pretribulation rapture or Postribulation rapture. Both groups of Christians believe the Bible. Both have Bible verses that they claim support their views of endtime events. The truth is, however, that how they understand key Bible verses is *entirely determined by the worldview they previously have embraced.*

We can make a comparison. People familiar with computers know that there are both IBM-compatible computers and Apple computers. Certain programs can be run on IBM computers and others on Apple computers. In similar fashion, the Pretribulational Premillennial scenario of events fits into the dispensational worldview. The Postribulational Premillennial scenario of events fits into the restorational worldview.

Therefore, when dispensational Christians talk to restorational Christians about endtime events, or vice versa, they really are challenging each others' worldview.

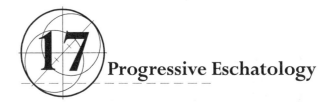

17 Progressive Eschatology

I commend the restorationalists and the Pentecostals for their improvements on dispensational thinking, but they did not go far enough. We must recognize the times when God intervened in history; however, rather than thinking of each intervention as a beginning and an end of a dispensation, we should see each intervention as another step forward in God's unfolding plan. He "...works all things after the counsel of His will" (Eph. 1:11). His actions are progressive steps, each leading to the summation of all things in Christ Jesus.

The Progressive Worldview

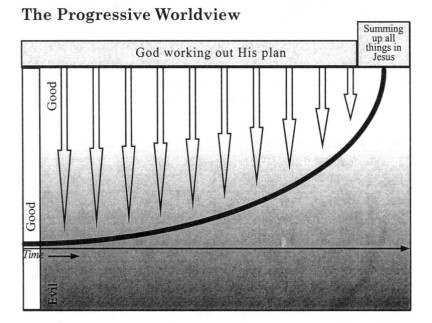

Bringing the Future into Focus

Only if we think in this progressive way can we develop an accurate view of endtime events.

I will take the next several chapters to discuss the progressive Christian's understanding of how the future will unfold. However, I must develop this picture in a clear, careful manner because so many Christians have been exposed only to the dispensational and/or restorational views. I believe that the concepts which logically follow from the progressive worldview are the most accurate biblically.

The foundational understanding of the progressive worldview is that God is unfolding His plan throughout the ages in a step-by-step fashion. Everything God ever has spoken will be fulfilled. The Church will arise to a place of maturity and glory (much greater than She experienced on Pentecost Day) and in the end, everything will be brought into submission to Jesus Christ.

If I were to end this book right now, or if you were to close it and never read another page, yet still embrace the progressive worldview, you eventually would arrive at an understanding of the future very similar to the picture I will present. Just as there is a scenario of endtime events that fits dispensationalism and another that fits restorationalism, so also there is a scenario that logically follows from the progressive worldview.

As we investigate this, keep in mind that there is a difference between a worldview and an eschatological view. A worldview is the whole picture a person has of Creation, history, the Church, the future, society, and the entire world around us. Eschatology is a study or belief system for endtime events. One's worldview and eschatology are interrelated, yet eschatology is only a small part—the end part—of the whole picture.

We have been studying three worldviews: dispensational, restorational, and progressive. As I explained, studying the Bible through dispensational eyes leads to the Pretribulational, Premillennial eschatology. The restorational worldview leads to the Postribulational, Premillennial eschatology. The progressive worldview also leads to a certain eschatological understanding, which I am in the process of defining.

WORLDVIEW————————>LEADS TO————————>	ESCHATOLOGY
DISPENSATIONAL————————————————————>	PRETRIBULATIONAL PREMILLENIAL
RESTORATIONAL————————————————————>	POSTRIBULATIONAL PREMILLENIAL
PROGRESSIVE————————————————————>	?

Readers who already are studied in eschatology may read the following pages trying to match my understanding to views held by various Christian groups. Indeed, there are three major eschatological views (other than the two which we already have discussed) held by Christians today. They are called Historic Premillennialism, Amillennialism, and Postmillennialism. Those familiar with these views will read the discussion in the following pages and be able to see some similarities and some dissimilarities with each of these eschatological views. However, I will not be aligning the progressive view with any one of them completely.

Progressive View of the Church

The eschatological views which match our three worldviews are very much determined by their own unique view of the Church and how She will be in the future. Dispensationalists see the Church being a stable entity (perhaps changing in size, but not in character or quality), "holding the fort" against an evil, advancing world. The restorationists see the ondtime Church as a purified remnant, resembling the Church on Pentecost Day. The progressive view declares that the Church, as a whole, will arise to glory, unity, and maturity before the return of Jesus Christ.

I believe the progressive vision of the Church most clearly matches the description Paul gives in the book of Ephesians:

> ...the whole building, being fitted together
> is growing into a holy temple in the Lord;
> in whom you also are being built together
> into a dwelling of God in the Spirit.
> (Eph. 2:21-22)

God is building something on Earth. It is being made from us, His people. Paul said that the Church "...is growing into a holy temple in the Lord" (Eph. 2:21). We are being fitly framed together to be a place for God to dwell. Of course, God is with His people now;

however, God is building a place for Himself to come and dwell in greater fullness. As Paul said, this building is being constructed for "...a dwelling of God in the Spirit" (Eph. 2:22).

This building project was prophesied throughout the Old Testament (i.e., I Chron. 17:12) and it has been under construction since the Church was birthed through Jesus Christ. Our Lord declared:

> "...I will build My church; and the gates
> of Hades shall not overpower it."
>
> (Matt. 16:18)

Jesus will succeed. He will continue building the Church until He completes the task and arrives at His goal.

The goal He has for the Church is unity and maturity. The apostle Paul explained in the book of Ephesians that Jesus planted leaders in the Church to equip the saints:

> ...to the building up of the body of Christ;
> until we all attain to the unity of the
> faith, and of the knowledge of the Son of
> God, to a mature man, to the measure of
> the stature which belongs to the fullness
> of Christ.   (Eph. 4:12-13)

Notice the goal: unity of the faith, knowledge of the Son of God, and maturity. Jesus will keep building until this goal is attained.

Progressive View of the Church

This glorious image of the future Church is shared by restorational and progressive Christians; however, they have a few distinctives. In addition to seeing the future Church as *much greater* than She appeared on Pentecost Day, progressive Christians envision the *whole* Church arising. In contrast, the restorationalists believe only a *remnant* of the Church will arise in glory.

Also, the *pathway* through which the Church shall mature is understood differently by the restorationalist and progressive Christian. Restorationalist envision a difficult path with great trials in our future. The progressive worldview recognizes some trials in our future, but not as intense nor as serious as the restorationists does. This distinction will take some time to develop, but we will begin with the next chapter.

The Coming Great Tribulation?

Restorationalists like to quote Isaiah 60:2:

*"For behold, darkness will cover the
 earth,
And deep darkness the peoples;
But the Lord will rise upon the you,
And His glory will appear upon you. "*

When restorationalists teach from this verse, they typically offer a view of the world getting much worse, but God purifying, refining, and glorifying His Church in the midst of increasing darkness.

Progressive Christians have a different view of the future. They see the Church arising in glory, but they also see the Church having a dramatic impact upon the world, and hence, changing the world into a better place. God is successfully working out His will in the Earth. The whole world is being dramatically transformed. The Kingdom of God is advancing in the Earth.

This more optimistic view will be developed throughout the remaining portion of this book. In this chapter, I must undermine the doctrine of a coming Great Tribulation.

Most restorationalists and the dispensationalists believe a worldwide seven-year long Tribulation is ahead of us. As we discussed earlier, they envision

Bringing the Future into Focus

Satan's activity increasing in the world, the Antichrist rising to power, and a false religious system coming against the true Church. They think one evil government will arise to oppress Christians and Jews. During that period there will be famines, diseases, financial disaster, earthquakes, destruction of the environment, and intense persecution. These and other catastrophic difficulties will increase as people reap the consequences of their own sins. God will also judge the world and He will eventually pour out His wrath upon humanity.

In contrast, the progressive worldview does not envision a future seven-year Tribulation. There are several reasons.

First of all, the idea of God pouring out His wrath upon the world is in direct contradiction to the covenant He established with Noah. After the flood, God spoke to Noah, saying:

> *"I will never again curse the ground on account of man...."* (Gen. 8:21)

After making this promise, God went on to further declare that as long as the Earth remains, there will be seasons, planting, and harvesting. He expounded upon His promise, talking about plants and animals being given as food (Gen. 9:1-3). God established this covenant with Noah and all of his descendants after him (Gen. 9:9). We are assured that it is an "everlasting covenant" (Gen. 9:16).

Dispensationalists and restorationalists envision God soon devastating the Earth. They justify this by redefining God's promise to Noah and saying that it only means He will avoid *using a flood* to destroy the Earth. Without realizing it, dispensationalists teach that God will soon break the everlasting covenant He made to "never again curse the ground."

In contrast, Christians with a progressive worldview believe God will keep *all of His covenants*. This is the very foundation of the progressive worldview. Every covenant and every act of God is valid and progressively building toward the summing up of all things in Jesus. Hence, progressive Christians do not believe God will pour out His wrath on the Earth.

This may surprise those who have been grounded in Dispensational or Restorational Premillennialism. In most of those circles, a coming Tribulation is talked about so much that they typically assume every Christian believes in it. In fact, some hold the validity of this doctrine on an equal level to the central aspects of the Gospel, such as the fact that Jesus died for our sins. Of course, valuing the two doctrines on an equal level is foolish, yet thousands of Evangelical Christians today hold to the doctrine of a coming Great Tribulation so tightly that to question its validity is to question something very sacred to them.

The doctrine of a coming Great Tribulation is primarily taught using two passages of the Bible: Matthew 24 and Revelation 4-19. Later I will briefly show the Book of Revelation in the progressive perspective. Here let me discuss Matthew 24.

In that chapter, Jesus told of coming wars, rumors of war, famines, and earthquakes. Our Lord went on to talk about people falling away from the faith, an abomination of desolation standing in the holy place, and then a great destruction from which people will have to flee (Matt. 24:6-21).

Dispensational teachers use this passage much more frequently than restorationalists to warn the Church of future troubles and a coming Tribulation. The restorational teachers tend to build their view of coming destruction upon the Book of Revelation.

In reality, most of the Christian leaders around the world today (and throughout Church history) believe(d) that the tribulation discussed in Matthew, chapter 24, happened between 40 and 70 AD. Between 64 and 68 AD, the Emperor Nero ordered a violent and aggressive persecution of Jews and Christians. Between 67 and 70 AD, a 42-month-long war was waged between the Jews and Rome, ending in the destruction of Jerusalem.*

Josephus, the most known historian of that time, described how Jerusalem was cut off from all outside sources of food. Thousands of Jews starved to death. Those who tried to escape were tortured, many had their hands cut off, and for an extended period approximately 500 Jews were crucified every day. More than a million Jews were slaughtered. Over 8,000 had their throats slit in the Temple. The city of Jerusalem and the Temple were left in ruins.**

To see the 70 AD destruction of Jerusalem as the fulfillment of our Lord's prophecy, we must see Matthew 24 in its context. Throughout chapter 23

---

* Many noted restorational teachers (i.e., Dr. Bill Hamon in his book, *The Eternal Church*) also teach that the tribulation talked about in Matthew 24:6-21 occurred in 70 AD.

** Josephus, *The War of the Jews*, v:x:3; v:xi:1-2; vi:iii:3-4; vi:iv.

The Coming Great Tribulation?

Jesus was speaking harsh words of judgment over the Jewish religious leaders. He ended His declaration saying that their Temple would be left desolate (Matt. 23:38). Then as He withdrew from the Temple, He looked back with His disciples, and He said to them:

> *"Do you see all these things? Truly I say to you, not one stone here shall be left upon another, which will not be torn down."*   (Matt. 24:2)

The Temple at which they were looking, indeed, was destroyed in 70 AD.

Dispensational Premillennialists rarely talk about these historical facts, but if these facts are brought to their attention, they quickly assert that we should expect another—even a greater—destruction which shall cover the whole world in the future.

Christian teachers who believe that the destruction foretold in Matthew 24:5-21 was fulfilled in 70 AD point out that Jesus told the disciples that the destruction would be in their region around Jerusalem (Matt. 24:16), and that it would happen within their generation. He sandwiched His prophecy between two key statements indicating the time frame:

> *"Truly I say to you, all these things shall come upon this generation."* (Matt. 23:36)

> *"Truly I say to you, this generation will not pass away until all these things take place."*   (Matt. 24:34)

Bringing the Future into Focus

If, indeed, the destruction of which is spoken in Matthew 24:5-21 happened within the lifetime of the people who actually were standing in our Lord's physical presence, then we should not think He was speaking of a Tribulation which will happen in our future.*

Once again, I need to say that this understanding of Matthew 24:5-21 can be disturbing to Christians who have been exposed only to dispensational thinking. Hearing that the tribulation of Matthew 24 is already fulfilled is most alarming to Evangelical Christians living in the United States, because they have been grounded in Dispensational Premillennialism. They, more than any other group, have been bombarded with books and television shows based on the doctrine of a coming Tribulation.

In truth, most of the Church worldwide today does *not* believe that the tribulation talked about in Matthew 24 is ahead of us. Nor has this doctrine been held by most of the influential leaders throughout the last 2,000 years of Church history.**

---

* Some teachers interpret the word *generation* in Matthew 24:34 to mean *race* (from the Greek, *gennema*), hence, they say that our Lord's Words will come to pass in our future, before the Jewish race is destroyed. The opposing argument is that no where else in the Scriptures is this Greek word interpreted as *race*. Therefore, to say that it means race here is to twist the meaning of Scripture to make it fit into the doctrine of a future Tribulation.

** In addition to many modern Evangelical teachers, most theologians of the mainline denominations, such as Roman Catholic, Orthodox, Lutheran, Episcopalian, Presbyterian, Methodist, etc., do not believe in a future Great Tribulation. Nor did most of the Church fathers such as Augustine, Thomas Aquinas, Martin Luther, John Calvin, and Charles Spurgeon.

92

The Coming Great Tribulation?

I have touched only briefly on this subject, but there are hundreds of books today on each side of the argument. Countless books are on the shelves of our Christian bookstores explaining how the Tribulation in Matthew 24 soon will come upon us. There are also hundreds of books explaining how the troubles of Matthew 24 were fulfilled at the destruction of Jerusalem in 70 AD. I will not take the time to repeat those writings. Instead, I have listed a few good references in the appendix for those interested in investigating these subjects further.* However, I need to make the reader who lives in the United States aware of the fact that most of the popular Christian bookstores in our country do not carry books which present views other than ones teaching a coming Great Tribulation. They are very biased in presenting the Dispensational Premillennial view, in spite of the fact that it is the minority view from the perspective of the Church worldwide.

In challenging the doctrine of a coming Great Tribulation, I do not mean to say that there will not be *difficult times ahead.* People will continue to reap the consequences of their actions, and we live in a world where bad things happen. Throughout history God has used trials and difficulties to test, discipline, and refine His people. Even Jesus learned obedience from the things He suffered (Heb. 5:8). The progressive worldview recognizes that there will be trials and struggles for the Church until the day Jesus returns. In fact, there will be increasing struggles between righteousness and unrighteousness because both are

---

* I also have a set of teaching tapes available on this subject. Information on how to obtain these is in the Appendix.

growing in the Earth. However, as a Christian with a progressive worldview, I do not believe that there will be a seven-year period in the future during which God will pour out His wrath upon this world.

The Progressive Worldview Including Conflicts Between Righteousness and Unrighteousness

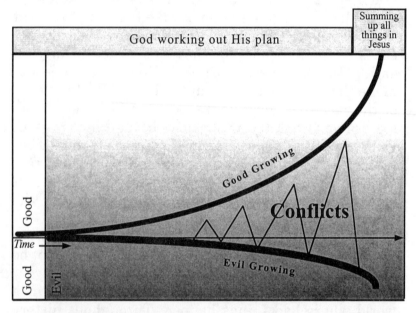

Sometimes Christians discuss their beliefs on when the rapture will take place in reference to the Tribulation. They will say they are "Pretrib" (Rapture before the Tribulation) or "Postrib" (Rapture after the Tribulation). Some even jokingly say that they are "Pan-Trib," meaning they don't care because it will all "pan out in the end."

I am "No-Trib." Future trials? Yes. Future Great Tribulation? No. Please let me continue telling why I believe this.

The Kingdom of God

God not only is building the Church, but also a Kingdom. When God gave His promise to King David, He said,

> "...I will set up one of your descendants after you, who will establish his kingdom. He shall build for Me a house, and I will establish his throne forever....I will settle him in My house and in My kingdom forever...."   (I Chron. 17:11-14)

Notice God promised to build two things: a house and a Kingdom.

All Christians believe in this Kingdom, but they understand it in different ways.

Christians trained with a dispensational or restorational worldview believe in a natural kingdom over which the Jews ruled in the Old Testament times. They see that as different from the Kingdom of God which was established *in heaven* 2,000 years ago. They believe the Kingdom of God will come down to the Earth at the Second Coming of Jesus in a catastrophic intervention. At that time Jesus will abolish evil and then establish His Kingdom on Earth for a 1,000-year period. As we have stated, they are "Premillennial," meaning Jesus will return before the Kingdom comes to Earth for a Millennium.

Both Dispensational and Restorational Christians are Premillennial

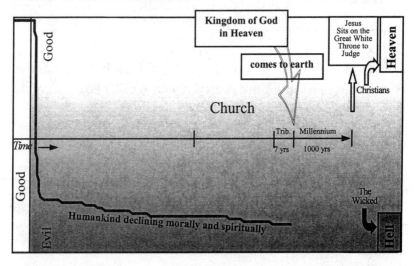

In contrast, Christians with a progressive worldview declare that Jesus is "sitting on the throne of David" (Is. 9:6-7). They see that the Kingdom of God was promised throughout the Old Testament and established when He sat down at the right hand of the Father. At that time, Jesus received all authority over heaven and Earth (Matt 28:18). Since the day He sat down on His throne, the Kingdom has extended over heaven *and Earth*. Therefore, Jesus has reigned over both heaven and Earth for 2,000 years. He presently is ruling from the throne located in heaven.

John the Baptist, the disciples, and Jesus declared, "The Kingdom of God is at hand!" They were announcing that the Kingdom of God had arrived, it was in reach. It was time for the prophecies concerning the Kingdom to be fulfilled.

The Progressive Understanding Showing Jesus Ruling from Heaven

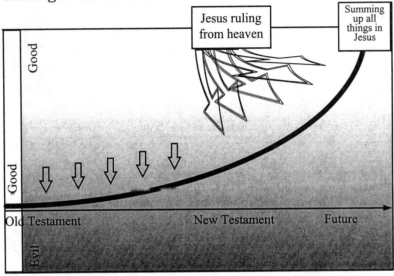

Progressive Christians believe that while we are on Earth, we have a dynamic and involved relationship with the Kingdom of God. The Apostle Paul explained that the Kingdom of God is "...righteousness and peace and joy in the Holy Spirit" (Rom. 14:17). He also taught that the Kingdom consists in power (I Cor. 4:20). The progressive Christian understands that these benefits—righteousness, peace, joy, and power—can be experienced now.

In contrast, Premillennialism teaches that the Kingdom of God is in heaven now, and, therefore, Christians will experience it after death or after it comes down to Earth during the Millennium.

Some dispensationalists teach that we can experience the Kingdom now, but only in a very limited way.

Bringing the Future into Focus

They say Christians are citizens of the Kingdom of God; however, that Kingdom is far away in heaven, and Christians are foreigners down here waiting to go home. As a foreigner still has some rights derived from his home country, so also a Christian on Earth may experience the Kingdom of God in some limited fashion. However, that experience is realized only within the heart of the Christian.

In contrast, Christians with a progressive worldview believe that we can have a much fuller experience of the Kingdom of God now while we are alive on Earth. Not only is a heart-felt experience of the Kingdom possible, but the literal authority of Jesus Christ can be manifested through our lives. Furthermore, as Christians, we can be active citizens of the Kingdom of God, functioning to release the King's will into the world around us today.

21 The Progression of the Kingdom

A progressive worldview leads us to believe that the Kingdom of God was promised throughout the Old Testament and established 2,000 years ago when Jesus sat down on His throne. Since that day the Kingdom of God has been growing similar to a seed (Matt. 13:24). The Kingdom also grows as yeast buried in dough (Matt. 13:33). A living cell divides in two, then four, then eight, then sixteen, then thirty-two, etc. This is exponential growth. The more time that passes, the more rapidly growth takes place.

This is how the progressive Christian sees the Kingdom of God growing on Earth. The seeds of the Kingdom have been planted throughout history. They "sprouted" 2,000 years ago when Jesus came.

Here is good news: the seeds of the Kingdom will grow until their presence is known throughout the whole world. Isaiah the prophet tells us this, saying,

> *There will be no end to the increase of His*
> *government or of peace,*
> *On the throne of David and over his*
> *kingdom,*
> *To establish it and to uphold it with*
> *justice and righteousness*
> *From then on and forevermore.*
> *The zeal of the Lord of hosts will*
> *accomplish this.* (Is. 9:7)

Bringing the Future into Focus

It is inevitable. Nothing can stop it. God will establish the authority of His Son. There will be no end to the increase of His government. It is a progressive takeover in process.

The Progressive Understanding of the Kingdom of God Growing in the Earth

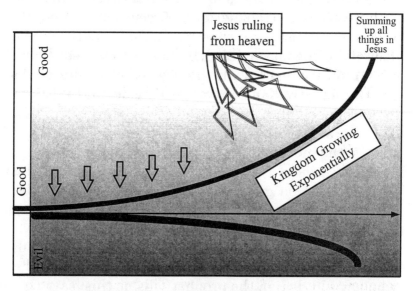

In order to embrace this progressive understanding, we must recognize that *authority* and *control* are two different things. To see this distinction, picture a king ruling over a natural kingdom. The king has *authority* throughout his kingdom, but that does not mean he is *controlling* everything in his kingdom. There may be rebels within his realm of authority, and there may be communities of people living contrary to the will of the king. At any time the king can come and squelch the rebellion because he has the authority to do it. However, just because he has the authority does not mean he is using his authority to control everything.

In a parallel fashion, Jesus has all authority over heaven and Earth. His Kingdom encompasses all, and it has for 2,000 years. He has been exalted above every other authority. However, Jesus is not using His authority to control everything. He could if He wanted to because He has the power to "subject all things to Himself" (Phil. 3:21). Yes, He has the authority and power, but He is not using it to control everything yet.

The Apostle Paul explained this relationship bo tween the authority and control of Jesus, saying:

For He must reign until He has put all of His enemies under His feet.
(I Cor. 15:25)

Jesus has been reigning over heaven and Earth for 2,000 years. He will continue sitting on His throne until a day comes when every knee bows and every tongue confesses Him as Lord. Then He will control all.

The progressive Christian would say that Jesus already has used His authority and taken control in heaven; however, He is using His authority and taking control of the Earth in a progressive fashion. For this reason we pray, Thy Kingdom come, Thy will be done on Earth as it is in heaven." Already His perfect will is being done in heaven. Now we are praying for Him to further His Kingdom, that is the King's will, on Earth.

Bringing the Future into Focus

The expansion of the Kingdom is not being done independently of the Church. Rather, Jesus is and will be taking control of this world with the cooperation of the people of God. Jesus already has given to the Church the *keys* to the Kingdom (Matt. 16:18-19), meaning we presently have the authority to release and activate King Jesus' authority on Earth. The closer we approach the return of our Lord, the more we will realize and access the authority given to us. Jesus, along with His Church, will release the King's will throughout the Earth.

Jesus explained that the Kingdom of God is like a mustard seed which grows to be the largest plant in the garden, even a tree (Matt. 13:31-32). We should expect this. The Kingdom of God will grow to be the single most influential entity on Earth.

Daniel, the prophet, revealed to us the same truth when he interpreted a dream of King Nebuchadnezzar. Several hundred years before Jesus came to Earth, God revealed to King Nebuchadnezzar what was going to take place with natural kingdoms and then the establishment of God's Kingdom.

In his dream, King Nebuchadnezzar saw a statue with four distinct parts. It had a head made of gold, a breast and arms of silver, a belly and thighs of bronze, and legs and feet of iron mixed with clay. In the dream, a stone came and struck the statue and crushed it. Then the rock grew into a great mountain and filled the whole Earth (Dan. 2:31-35).

Daniel explained the dream to King Nebuchadnezzar telling him that the four parts of the statue represented four kingdoms on Earth. Daniel told the king that his kingdom was the first, but three king-

doms would come after his. Indeed, we know histori-
cally that King Nebuchadnezzar ruled over Babylon.
The Medo-Persian kingdom followed his, then the
Greek empire, and finally the Roman Empire.

The most interesting point for our discussion has
to do with the promise of a rock which then came and
crushed the four kingdoms:

> *And in the days of these kings the God of
> heaven will set up a kingdom which will
> never be destroyed, and that kingdom
> will not be left for another people; it will
> crush and put an end to all these king-
> doms, but it will itself endure forever.*
>
> (Dan. 2:44)

Two thousand years ago during the Roman Empire,
the *Rock* came to Earth. God set up an eternal Kingdom which never shall be destroyed.

Daniel explained that God's eternal Kingdom will
grow until it becomes a great mountain and then fills
the whole Earth. He told the king:

> *"...God has made known to the king what
> will take place in the future...."*
>
> (Dan. 2:45)

This is inevitable. The future is assured. God has
established His King on His throne and that Kingdom
will expand until it has conquered all and filled all.

The zeal of the Lord of hosts will accomplish this.
It shall happen. It is happening.

Progressive Manifestation of Glory

As the Church and the Kingdom advance, the glory of God will manifest progressively in the Earth. This has been God's plan from the beginning. After Adam and Eve sinned, they hid from the presence of God. They were cast out of the Garden of Eden and no longer experienced immediate communion with God. Though the relationship was violated, God did not abandon humanity nor the rest of Creation. He repeatedly revealed Himself and has been doing it in a progressive fashion.

In the early books of the Bible we read about God revealing Himself to specific individuals. Enoch walked with God and God made a covenant with Noah. Abraham experienced God and Moses first encountered God when He spoke from out of a burning bush.

It was not until Moses led the Hebrew people out of Egypt that God revealed Himself to a group of people. God made His presence known to the Egyptians and Hebrew people through many signs and wonders. Though the Hebrew people were not allowed to see God, God came down and revealed some of His glory to them from Mount Sinai. He also led the people with a cloud by day and a pillar of fire by night. During the time that Moses met with God, the people were allowed to see the glory of God reflected upon the face of Moses.

Bringing the Future into Focus

God further revealed Himself as His presence was manifested from within the ark of the covenant. Several times the cloud of God's glory enveloped the tent and the elders of the people.

As the Hebrew people took over the Promised Land, God's presence repeatedly was made known, first to the Jews, but also to the surrounding nations as they became aware of God's presence among the Hebrews. When Solomon built the Temple in Jerusalem, God's glory filled it, though God made it clear that He could not be contained within a building.

Though God withdrew His presence as the Jews forsook Him, He sent prophets promising of a future day when His presence would be known even more fully. That day came when the Word became flesh and dwelt among us. History changed when Jesus declared to His disciples, "He who has seen Me has seen the Father" (John 14:9). Then through His death and resurrection, the Son was glorified by the Father. That glory has been declared progressively over the Earth.

A day will come when Jesus will return and be revealed to the whole world in His full glory. Then all of the nations will bow in His presence.

Between the First and Second Coming of our Lord, He is being revealed through the Holy Spirit. This, too, is a progressive revelation. The Spirit has been released into the hearts of God's people. This was an unparalleled advancement over the availability of the Spirit in the Old Testament times when only a few individuals experienced the presence of the Holy Spirit. After Jesus ascended, the Spirit was poured out and began to flow as rivers from the innermost being of those who believed in Him (John 7:38-39). That flow increases as the Church advances over the face of the Earth. Before the end the Spirit will be poured out upon *all* humankind.

Christians have become the Temple of God; a dwelling place of His Spirit. Though the Church has had times of glory and times of faltering, Jesus is building His Church, and He will continue doing so until we, as a people, have attained to "the knowledge of the Son of God, to a mature man, to the measure of the stature which belongs to the fullness of Christ" (Eph. 4:13).

God is making Himself a dwelling place. He is coming to Earth! Not only will His presence be contained within His people, but they shall be made a light to the nations, a city set on a hill, a beacon for all humanity.

The glory of the Lord shall shine forth and fill the Earth. The prophets in the Old Testament spoke of this day. The Psalm writer called it forth saying:

> *And blessed be His glorious name forever;*
> *And may the whole earth be filled with*
> *His glory.*
> *Amen, and Amen.* (Ps. 72:19)

Habakkuk assured us it would happen:

> *"For the earth will be filled*
> *With the knowledge of the glory of the*
> *Lord,*
> *As the waters cover the sea."* (Hab. 2:14)

Bringing the Future into Focus

God Himself declared to Moses:

> *"...as I live, all the earth will be filled with the glory of the Lord."*
>
> (Num. 14:21)

It is inevitable, inescapable, destined to happen. God is in the process of revealing Himself. He progressively is manifesting His glory, and, in the end, His glory will fill this entire Earth.

 **The Return of Jesus Christ**

If we study the Bible from the progressive perspective, we will conclude that the Church will rise to unity and maturity, the Kingdom of God will continue to advance, the glory of God will fill the Earth, and Jesus Christ will return.

It is helpful to identify at what point Jesus will return. No one knows the exact day; however, there are several Bible passages which give us an idea concerning the timing of the Second Coming.

Peter wrote:

> *The Lord is not slow about His promise,*
> *as some count slowness, but is patient*
> *toward you, not wishing for any to perish*
> *but for all to come to repentance.*
>
> (I Peter 3:9)

I offer this to you as the single most profound factor determining when our Lord will return—when the Father is satisfied with the salvation of people. As a farmer watches over his crops to see when they come to maturity before he brings in the harvest, so God is watching over the Earth, and He will not release the Son until He is satisfied with the fullness of the harvest.

This contrasts with Dispensational Premillennialists who center their predictions of the Second Coming around a host of negative catastrophic events: earth-quakes, wars, famine, disease, destruction of the envi-ronment, the Antichrist, etc. The Christian with a progressive worldview sees God's patience, lov-ingkindness, and desire for more people to be saved determining the Second Coming—rather than His ability to restrain His own wrath which soon will be poured out upon this world.

Another important fact, which we must add to our understanding about the timing of the Second Coming is that evil still will be in the world when Jesus returns.

Our Lord told a parable teaching about the King-dom, saying:

> *"...it may be compared to a man who sowed good seed in his field. But while men were sleeping, his enemy came and sowed tares also among the wheat, and went away. But when the wheat sprang up and bore grain, then the tares became evident also."* (Matt. 13:24-26)

The field is the Earth. The good seeds are growing. However, an enemy has been planting bad seeds which also are growing. Jesus explained that both the good and bad seeds will grow to maturity and then:

> *"...in the time of the harvest I will say to the reapers, "First gather up the tares and bind them in bundles to burn up; but gather the wheat into my barn."'"* (Matt. 13:30)

Notice that in the time of harvest both good and bad seeds will have grown to maturity, and then they will be separated from each other (see also Matt. 25:31-46). Yes, good and evil will be present when Jesus returns for the harvest.

Some Christians overlook this truth. They learn about the Church arising to maturity and glory, and they become so excited about this truth that they envision Her subduing all evil before the return of Jesus Christ. This is called, Dominion Theology, a view which I am *not* promoting. I believe that the Church and the Kingdom of God are headed in the *direction of dominion*; however, they will not conquer all evil in the world before Jesus returns. Both good and evil will mature. The Church will arise to maturity; however, maturity does not mean She will subdue all evil. She will mature in the midst of both good and evil growing. It will take the appearance of Jesus Christ to do the final separation of the the tares from the wheat.

Dominion Theology minimizes or even denies the coming "Day of our Lord." There are several Bible passages which describe a future day when Jesus will put an end to evil by the power of His appearing. If we wrongly envision the Church subduing all evil and then Jesus returning, we eliminate that glorious day when Jesus will exercise a great judgment upon the evil remaining in the world.

We must see the return of Jesus as another progressive step in God's unfolding plan. The Kingdom of God is advancing, the Church is maturing, and one day Jesus will return to judge the world and reveal His glory. It will take the exertion of His power to put a final end to evil and establish His perfect will throughout the world. When Jesus appears, every enemy will bow at *His* feet and confess *Him* as Lord.

The Progressive Worldview Showing the Return of Jesus

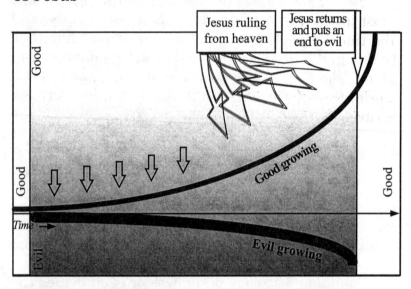

Jesus gave us another parable revealing this truth:

> *"The kingdom of heaven is like a mustard seed, which a man took and sowed in his field; and this is smaller than all other seeds; but when it is full grown, it is larger than the garden plants, and becomes a tree, so that the birds of the air come and nest in its branches."*
>
> (Matt. 13:31-32)

The Kingdom began as a seed, first as promises of God given throughout the Old Testament, then manifesting as Jesus came to Earth. That seed has grown over all the Earth, and eventually it will become the largest of all trees in the garden.

Yes, the Kingdom of God will be the largest, the most influential force in all of the world. However, at the time of our King's return there still will be other plants in the garden—the enemy also has planted his seeds. The Kingdom of God will grow to dominate the world; however, evil also will remain here until Jesus returns for the final judgment.

The Jews and the Kingdom

The role and future position of the Jews is another key in understanding the Kingdom of God.

Dispensational and Restorational Premillennialists believe that the Great Tribulation and Millennium are set aside by God so that He can fulfill the promises to the Jews which He made in the Old Testament. They believe that God is dealing with the Gentiles during the present "Church Age," and when this dispensation comes to a close, God will turn His favor back to the Jews. When the Kingdom of God comes to Earth, Gentiles will be present and blessed, yet the Jews will receive a place of authority, favor, and honor.

Premillennialists also teach that preceding the Millennium (during the Tribulation and the few years before it) the nation of Israel will be restored, Jews living throughout the world will migrate back to the Promised Land, the temple in Jerusalem will be rebuilt, and sacrifices will be offered in the temple. Then toward the end of the seven-year Tribulation, a war will break out (called Armageddon) in which several mighty nations will come against Israel. However, God will reveal His choice of the Jewish people by supernaturally causing them to win the great battle, making them victorious over all of their enemies. In the midst of that battle, Jesus Christ will return and establish His Kingdom on Earth, giving the Jews a prominent place of rulership over the whole world for 1,000 years.

The Premillennial (Dispensational and Restorational) View Showing the Millennium Primarily for God to Show His Favor to the Jews

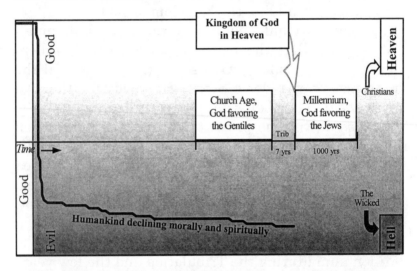

Progressive Christianity has a different perspective of the Jews. Before I explain this, I need to tell you what progressive Christianity does *not* teach.

There are some Christian groups which take a view at the opposite extreme from the dispensational view in reference to the Jews. They embrace "Replacement Theology." As we mentioned earlier, this view teaches that God rejected the Jews and replaced them with Christians. Replacement Theology says that the promises made to the Jews in the Old Testament, which were not fulfilled completely, will be fulfilled in the lives of His new chosen people.

The Jews and the Kingdom

I do not teach Replacement Theology. God still has a covenant with the Jews. In fact, *God's covenant has progressed and been enlarged to include Gentiles who believe in Jesus.*

Furthermore, the Kingdom over which Jesus rules is the same Kingdom which was promised to the Jews throughout the Old Testament. When Jesus came, He came as a descendant of David, and He is sitting "on the throne of David" (Is. 9:6-7). The throne of the Kingdom is not limited to Jerusalem on Earth but has been lifted into heaven into the new Jerusalem. When Jesus ascended, the Kingdom expanded to envelop heaven and Earth.

Christians holding to Replacement Theology often use Hebrews, chapters seven and eight, to teach their doctrine that God's covenant with the Jews has ended. In particular, they like to quote the following:

> *For if that first covenant had been fault-less, there would have been no occasion sought for a second....When He said, "A new covenant," He has made the first obsolete, but whatever is becoming obsolete and growing old is ready to disappear.* (Heb. 8:7-13)

At first glance, a reader may conclude from this passage that God has ended the covenant He established with the Jews. In reality, Hebrews seven and eight are not talking about the Abrahamic covenant, but rather the *religious system* God established through Moses, with animal sacrifices and people going to God through a high priest. *That religious system is obsolete* and it has been replaced by the sacrifice of Jesus on the cross, with Him as our high priest.

We must not confuse the Mosaic religious system, which is obsolete, with the Abrahamic covenant, which is not obsolete. The Abrahamic covenant was established more than four centuries before the Mosaic religious system. Furthermore, several passages of Scripture tell us that the covenant God made with Abraham and his descendants is an *eternal covenant* (i.e., Gen. 17:7, 13; I Chron. 16:16-17; Ps. 105:9-10).

The Jews still have a covenant with God. That did not change. However, the covenant God made with Abraham has been expanded, increased, improved, and offered to Gentiles through Jesus Christ (Gal. 3:7-14).

Those who follow Replacement Theology use another false argument to teach that God has rejected the Jews and replaced them with Christians. They quote a passage from the Old Testament in which God declared that He divorced Israel:

> *"And I saw that for all the adulteries of faithless Israel, I had sent her away and given her a writ of divorce...."* (Jer. 3:8)

To see that this passage does *not* mean God has divorced the Jews, we must realize that at the time of history this passage was written, the Jewish nation had been divided into two parts, referred to individually as Israel and Judah. Both Israel and Judah strayed into idolatry, and God said He gave *Israel a writ of divorce.* However, Judah—not Israel—carried the promise of a coming Kingdom. Judah is rightfully called the Jewish people. God did not divorce Judah. In fact, in this passage God was calling Judah back from her wickedness. In several other passages, God promised never to abandon Judah, no matter what she did (i.e., Is. 49:14-16).

The important point is that God still has a covenant with the Jews. As Paul wrote:

> *...God has not rejected His people, has He? May it never be! For I too am an Israelite, a descendant of Abraham, of the tribe of Benjamin. God has not rejected His people whom He foreknew...."*
>
> (Rom. 11:1-2)

God will fulfill His promises to the Jewish people.

God's covenant with the Jews is not only to establish them as a people, but to bless them if they are obedient and curse them if they are disobedient (Deut. 28). God's severe dealings with the Jews throughout history—both blessings and punishments—are evidence of His ongoing covenant.

Furthermore, the Jews have an ongoing covenant with God which ensures them a glorious future in the Kingdom of God. Throughout the last 2,000 years, only a remnant of the Jews have been experiencing the Kingdom. Paul explains in Romans 11 that God hardened them from recognizing Jesus as the Messiah. However, a day will come when God will open the eyes of the Jewish people, and they will accept

Jesus. Then Jews will come into the Kingdom of God in large numbers. In fact, Paul writes "...all Israel will be saved..." (Rom. 11:26).

When will this Jewish awakening happen? After the "fullness of the Gentiles has come in" (Rom. 11:25). Paul explained that after God has allowed a full season of harvest and is satisfied with the Gentiles who have come into His spiritual family, He will turn His favor to the Jewish people and reveal to them that Jesus is their Messiah.

The closer we get to the return of Jesus, the more we will see an incredible, supernatural awakening among the Jewish people. However, this future awakening will not be as the dispensationalists envision. The Jews will not go back to offering sacrifices and worshipping in their temple. Rather, they will accept Jesus Christ. They will come into the New Covenant. They will worship God with the Body of Christ. Jews and Gentiles shall become one flock with One Shepherd (John 10:16).

This is what Paul taught us in Ephesians, where he explained that Jesus:

> ...made both groups into one, and broke down the barrier of the dividing wall, by abolishing in His flesh the enmity, which is the Law of commandments, contained in ordinances, that in Himself He might make the two into one new man, thus establishing peace, and might reconcile them both in one body to God....
>
> (Eph. 2:14-16)

Paul further explains how God is building us, Jews and Gentiles, into one body, one temple, a dwelling place for His presence (Eph. 2:19-22).

This is the future of the Jews.

Progressive Understanding That Jews and Gentile Christians Shall Be Made One

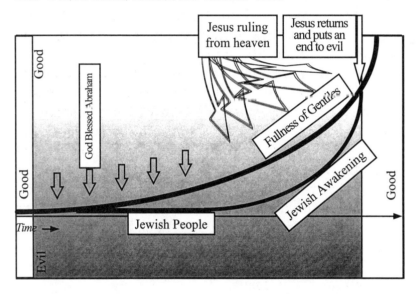

Dispensationalists wrongly see the Jews having a separate, distinct future from Christians. This is in accordance with the "dispensational way of thinking" which compartmentalizes time periods and people groups. It is easy for them to envision the Jews as a distinct, separate people with a future restoration of the Law, temple sacrifices, priesthood, etc.

Progressive Christianity believes that the religious system established through Moses has been made obsolete, and that God has *no intentions of restoring what He has ended.* Rather, the Jews will come into a major awakening, recognizing Jesus as the Messiah and being made one with the Church.

The Worldwide Revival Ahead

Progressive Christianity teaches that the greatest revival the world ever has seen is ahead of us.

Dispensationalists may shout, "Amen," when they hear a preacher promising a coming revival, but in reality, their worldview has *no room for it actually to occur.* Instead, dispensationalists are looking for the imminent return of Jesus, followed by seven years of the Great Tribulation. They believe that the world will get worse and worse because they think that the Tribulation and other events recorded in Matthew 24:4-21 are still ahead of us. To be consistent with their own doctrines, they must believe that preceding the Great Tribulation, lawlessness will increase, and most people's love will grow cold (Matt. 24:12). They do believe that the Gospel will be preached in the whole world before Jesus returns; however, they also must believe that simultaneously a great apostasy will come and many will fall away from the faith (Matt. 24:10). That belief is incompatible with the hope of a worldwide revival.

Restorationalists are not so pessimistic, because they have a hope for the remnant Church to get better. However, they see this happening as the world gets darker and darker. Some will talk about a coming revival, but it causes a conflict in their mind, because they still maintain that the world is headed downward. If they do believe in a future revival, they do not envision it as grand the progressive Christian does.

Bringing the Future into Focus

The dispensational worldview brings to prominence Scriptures which talk about war and destruction, increasing sin and death. In contrast, when a Christian studies the Bible through the progressive worldview, the Scripture verses which come to the forefront are the positive promises of God.

For example, progressive Christians like the promises recorded in Isaiah 19, which says:

> *Thus the Lord will make Himself known to Egypt, and the Egyptians will know the Lord in that day...In that day there will be a highway from Egypt to Assyria, and the Assyrians will come into Egypt and the Egyptians will worship with the Assyrians. In that day Israel will be the third party with Egypt and Assyria, a blessing in the midst of the Earth, whom the Lord of hosts has blessed, saying "Blessed is Egypt My people , and Assyria the work of My hands, and Israel My inheritance."*   (Is.19:21-24)

These verses have particular significance because Egypt and Assyria have been and still are the foundation of the Islamic religion. Today, one-fifth of the world's population is Muslim. Yet the Bible promises that Egypt and Assyria will worship the true God with Israel.

Progressive Christians see this being fulfilled in the coming revival before Jesus returns. Dispensational Premillennialists cannot place the fulfillment of these verses before Jesus returns because they envision the world getting worse and worse. Further, they believe that the enemies of Israel, in particular the Muslims, will become increasingly antagonistic toward Israel. Notice how our worldview leads us to have a positive or negative attitude toward Muslims.

Other people groups are looked at similarly. Dispensationalists believe Russia and China will also come against Israel toward the end of the Tribulation days. This leads Christians to interpret world events very differently. Consider the crumbling of the Soviet Union. Progressive Christians say that it was inevitable that communism lost its hold on much of the world, so we could effectively preach the Gospel and God could expand His Kingdom over the whole Earth. In contrast, dispensationalists believe Russia will soon turn against Israel and fight against God and His chosen people. Therefore, dispensationalists maintain a suspicion that Russia will turn against Jews and Christians at any time.

Similarly, dispensationalists think of China as the other major country which will come against Israel in the Tribulation days, fighting against God and His covenant people.

Dispensationalists may attempt to evangelize people in Russia and China, but they think we only have a short time to get the Gospel in before the doors close and terrible evil sweeps over those countries.

In contrast, progressive Christians believe that God is opening the whole world to the Gospel. They are looking for God to fulfill His promises to pour out His Spirit on all humanity (i.e., Joel 2:28). Not only will we preach to every group of people on the Earth, but the Arabs will respond to the Gospel and worship the true God. The people of Russia and China will come into a progressive revelation of Jesus Christ. Jews will have their eyes opened and recognize Jesus as their Messiah. Although evil will remain until Jesus returns, the majority of people will respond to the Gospel. The whole world will see the Church being made one. Division and strife within the Church will diminish. Signs and wonders will accompany this revival. The power of the Spirit will be present to convict of sin and unrighteousness. Millions, if not billions, will respond to the Gospel.

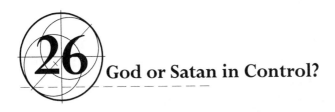

26 God or Satan in Control?

A fundamental difference between dispensationalism and the progressive worldview pertains to who is in charge of this world.

Dispensational Premillennialists (and to a lesser degree, Restorational Premillennialists) believe that Satan is extremely active in the world, and his influence will continually advance until it reaches a pinnacle in the endtimes. In fact, Premillennialists often emphasize that Satan is the "god of this world" (II Cor. 4:4). They teach that Satan is in control, and his kingdom will advance continually until it takes over almost all governments, finances, education, business, etc. This is in alignment with their view of the world sliding downhill, morally and spiritually, getting worse everyday.

This Premillennial belief of Satan's increasing activity is being aggressively promoted among the popular Christian culture (especially in America). Hundreds of books depict a dark, scary future. Televangelists come across the airwaves every day warning of impending doom. They say Satan soon will take over all or almost all governments in this world, and the Antichrist will deceive and rule the world. So terrible will conditions become that Christians will be persecuted to death. Active imaginations have embellished these stories and the endtime picture is that Satan's kingdom will grow until it overwhelms the Earth.

Bringing the Future into Focus

Although all Premillennialists would not give whole-hearted agreement to the popularized versions, they do envision Satan continually advancing his will and eventually taking control of the world up until the start of the Millennium.

The Premillennial View of Satan as God of This World and His Control Increasing in the Earth

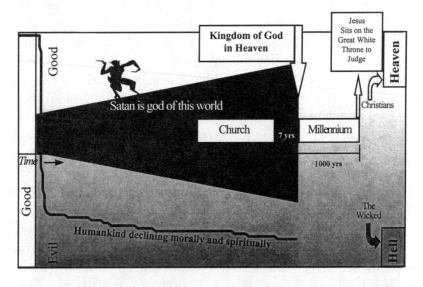

In contrast, Christians with a progressive world-view emphasize that Jesus is Lord. This may sound like a mere Christian cliché, but it has special significance to the progressive believer. Rather than saying Satan is god of this world, the progressive believer emphasizes that Jesus sat down on His throne 2,000 years ago, and He now rules over heaven and Earth. Satan and the whole Earth have been subjected to the Lordship of Jesus Christ.

The Progressive Worldview Showing Jesus as Lord

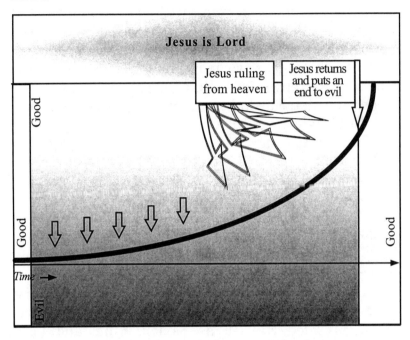

Progressive Christians may say that Satan is god of this world, but they would be using it in a derogatory manner, implying that Satan is a defeated enemy, no longer having authority in heaven and only able to influence people down here in a limited way. Furthermore, he only can blind the minds "of the unbelieving" (II Cor. 4:4). He has no legal authority over the believer, and the only power he can exercise is that which is allowed him. Jesus died "that through death He might render powerless him who had the power of death, that is, the devil" (Heb. 2:14). Satan *had* the power of death, but no longer. John tells us,

Bringing the Future into Focus

"The Son of God appeared for this purpose, that He might destroy the works of the devil" (I John 3:8b). Satan is no longer in control of this world. Jesus is Lord!

The progressive Christian envisions Satan's influence decreasing as we move into the future. Jesus Christ will reign until all of His enemies are put under His feet. The kingdoms of this world are becoming the Kingdoms of our God.

This issue comes down to who is in charge of this world: God or Satan? Of course, God has given humankind some authority in the Earth; however, we are asking the bigger question: Who is the over-lord?

Dispensationalists say that Jesus is Lord, yet they understand this phrase in a different way than progressive Christians. Dispensationalists often say "Jesus came as Savior the first time and He will come as King the next time." Progressive Christians disagree with this statement. Instead, they believe that Jesus revealed Himself as Savior, King, and Lord 2,000 years ago.

Humanity: Downhill or Uphill?

As I explained in the beginning of this study, both dispensational and restorational worldviews are built upon the foundational worldview of Reformed Theology. They each superimpose their unique view of history on the four major events: Creation, the Fall, Redemption, and the Consummation. Within that perspective, humankind is seen as locked onto a moral and spiritual decline.

The Worldview of Reformed Theology

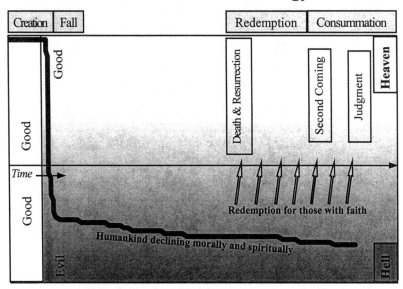

The progressive worldview also recognizes the four major events: Creation, the Fall, Redemption, and the Consummation. However, it is not locked into the view of humanity declining morally and spiritually. This allows us to form a more realistic and biblically-accurate view of humankind's moral and spiritual condition throughout the ages. Let's look at this, beginning with Adam and Eve, then quickly working our way into the present.

In the beginning God created the world and declared that it was good. Adam and Eve were created innocent (not knowing good from evil). However, after they ate of the forbidden fruit, sin entered the world. From that day forward, both good and evil were present, and humankind was able to choose between the two.

We do not have details recorded in the Bible of how morally good or bad Adam and Eve lived after the Fall. However, we do get a glimpse of the next generation—at least their first sons, Cain and Abel. Cain became so angry and jealous of Abel that he killed his brother. If we were to evaluate the moral conditions of humankind at that point, we would have to see it as very corrupt. As far as we know, no person had a revelation of the salvation which would come through Jesus Christ, and the only family on Earth of which we have record had a murderer in their midst.

This may seem simplistic, but compare humanity's moral condition then with humanity's condition today. Is the entire world in darkness concerning Jesus Christ today? No. Is there a literal murderer in the midst of every family on Earth today? No. Then we must recognize that the second generation of humankind was in a position of less spiritual enlightenment than humankind today.

Humanity: Downhill or Uphill?

If we study the Bible and follow the next several generations, we will see humankind's continued corruption. There are a few individuals, such as Enoch, who walked with God (Gen. 5:24), but by the time Noah came on the scene "the wickedness of man was great on the earth" (Gen. 6:5). Humanity reached a low point just before the flood with the whole world, except Noah, displeasing to God.

Immediately after the flood we see humankind still corrupted, yet in a better place spiritually than before the flood. At least Noah was seeking God. Yet that positive period did not last long. A few generations later we see the people building the Tower of Babel to make a name for themselves (Gen. 11:3-4). There may have been some who were seeking God, but secular history reveals that the vast majority of humankind was hedonistic, or involved in worshipping false gods, animals, their ancestors, or nature.

New hope was brought into the world when God made a covenant with Abraham. As Abraham's descendants multiplied, God repeatedly reached out to them, revealing Himself in various ways. There were times when the Jewish people followed God, and other times when they drifted into idol worship. Their moral and spiritual condition seemed to go up and down, usually corresponding to the righteousness or unrighteousness of the leadership at the time.

The general picture we get from the Old Testament is that only the tiny nation of Israel worshipped the true God, and even they sometimes backslid into Baal worship and following the other false gods of the surrounding nations.

Bringing the Future into Focus

Do not think the world then was better spiritually than it is now, especially since the clearest revelation of God—that is, through Jesus Christ—was not even given to humankind until the New Testament.

Two thousand years ago Jesus died and resurrected. The Church and the Kingdom began to grow as seeds. Since then there have been spiritual ups and downs in various places on the Earth. However, the Church and the Kingdom are growing.

How are we to understand this? Is the Reformed view of inevitable and inescapable moral and spiritual decline true?* No. In two obvious ways it is false.

First, people are not locked into a predetermined spiritual decline. They have a free will to reject or respond to God.

Second, there have been many times in history which have been much worse morally and spiritually than the present. (For example, people during the height of the Roman Empire were astonishingly corrupt.) The idea of inevitable decline is neither historically nor biblically accurate.

The progressive worldview goes further and declares that the world is—generally speaking—getting better. Both good and evil are growing in the Earth, but the Kingdom of God will become the largest and greatest influence on the Earth before Jesus returns.

The truth is that Christianity is already the largest religion in the world with one out of every

---

* Some Christian groups, such as the Puritans during the Eighteenth Century, held to Reformed Theology, yet developed a positive view for the future of humankind.

three people claiming to be Christian. Obviously we have a long way to go, but the progressive worldview teaches that good will continue growing until its presence is greater than evil.

The Progressive Worldview Showing the Moral and Spiritual Progress of Humanity

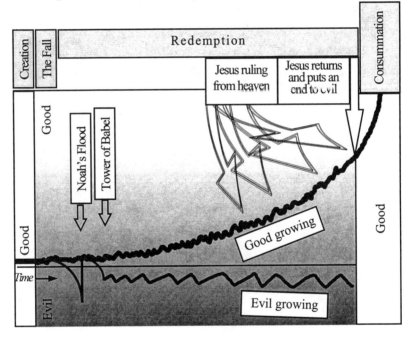

28 Thy Will Be Done on Earth

The progressive worldview sees things moving in a positive direction. It also sees every intervention of God as a progressive step in bringing forth God's will.

To embrace this view you must recognize God's will as greater than simply getting people to become Christians. What God is doing in the world is bigger. He is working inside and outside of the Church. When we pray to God, "Thy will be done on Earth as it is in heaven," we are asking Him to cause His will to fill and take over this entire world.

Consider this truth in reference to God's original blessing. When God blessed Adam and Eve, He released a force to cause humankind to fill and subdue the Earth. Notice that this has little to do with getting people to become Christians. Yet it is still God's will for humankind successfully to manage and live on the Earth. Therefore, when we talk about God's will progressively increasing in the Earth, we are not talking about only what He is doing inside the Church.

When a medical researcher finds a cure for a disease, he/she is furthering the will of God in the Earth. When an agricultural engineer finds new ways to produce food for people, he/she is accomplishing what God wants accomplished. When a police officer enforces the law, he/she is enforcing the will of God. As teachers instruct their students how to read, do mathematics, and prepare for a career, those students are being prepared to be successful in life, which is also God's desire for humanity. When people manage the Earth's resources well, they are doing the will of God.

Notice I am *not* saying that the individuals mentioned above are Christians. Nor am I saying that they will become Christians simply by doing good works. Nor am I saying that all progress is of God. *I am saying* that God wants humanity to live successfully, and He uses whomever He wants to work out His will in the Earth.

God loves the world. He wants to help and bless humanity. Think of this in the perspective of God sending His people into the world as salt. Salt is placed on meat to preserve it and make it flavorful. God not only is interested in the salt. He is interested in the meat. He is concerned about and loves the whole world. He sends His people into the world to help preserve them, bring them truth, and release His blessings. God's will entails much more than what God is doing in the Church.

God's blessing upon Abraham's life is another blessing which influences the whole Earth. The natural and spiritual descendants of Abraham have both the original blessing upon their lives and that which God gave to Abraham. Hence, they are more able, more empowered, more capable of bringing the will of God into the Earth. They have an additional blessing through which God will bless all of the families of the Earth.

When God gave the Law through Moses, He was further revealing His will. As Christians, we know that the related religious system was made obsolete, yet the expression of God's will to humanity remains a priceless treasure. God, Who is up in heaven, communicated with humankind and told us such things as "Worship Him alone" and "Honor thy father and mother." We are not in total darkness. God spoke to us.

When God promised David a future Kingdom, He was setting in motion His rulership over heaven and Earth. When God sent Jesus to die on the cross, He made provisions for the forgiveness of our sins. When God raised Jesus to sit at His right hand, He put a righteous and good Lord over everything. When the Holy Spirit was poured out, the power and guidance of God was made available to His children. Today, Jesus is building His Church, and it is being formed into a dwelling place for God's manifest presence. When Jesus literally returns, He will eliminate evil from the Earth.

All of these and the innumerable other works of God progressively work toward the summing up of all things in Jesus.

This means that all of God's works are "redemptive," even such interventions of God as the destruction which happened in Noah's day. Much evil was cleansed from the Earth, and what remained was a more righteous offspring left to repopulate the Earth. God was giving humanity another chance.

This is how Christians with a progressive worldview see the works of God. God is not interested only in Christians. He is working out His will throughout the whole of humanity. Everything He does is redemptive in nature.

The Progressive Worldview Showing All of God's Works as Redemptive

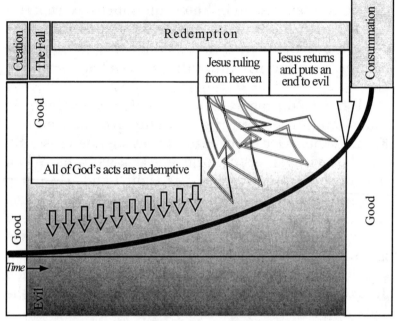

Christians grounded in Reformed Theology (Dispensational and Restorational Premillennialists) may give mental assent to this truth that all of God's works are redemptive, yet they do not fit the redemptive acts (outside of the death and resurrection of Jesus) into the overall workings of God throughout time. In line with the dispensational way of thinking, they tend to compartmentalize the works of God, applying them to specific people groups and specific time periods. They see God's acts in the Old Testament as failed attempts to help humankind or, at best, temporary aids. Even God's redemptive acts in Jesus Christ are seen as only the salvaging of a small percentage of humanity out of a huge, increasingly evil world.

At the very foundation of dispensationalism is a misunderstanding of Law and grace.* The major point of dispensational thought is a contrast between God's dealing with humankind during the Old Testament period versus His dealings in the present "Age of Grace." The labels themselves indicate the lack of understanding concerning how God is a God of grace in all times. The Christian with a progressive worldview sees every act of God throughout time as redemptive, and, hence, an act of grace. It is the progressive outpouring of God's grace which ensures for us a glorious future.

The Christian with a progressive worldview will say that God is not merely rescuing a people out of the world, but continually reaching out to and helping humankind as a whole. (This does not mean that every human being will be saved, for the judgment day will come when Jesus will separate the wicked from the righteous.)

God is interested in all Creation. He is not merely pulling a group of people out of Creation. Rather, He is eliminating evil from Creation and setting Creation free from corruption. God will bring all of Creation into submission to the Son.

Every time God speaks, His Words continue until they literally have produced what they have been sent to do. Dispensationalists and restorationalists do not have this understanding of God's work or Words. For

---

* Dr. Daniel Juster deserves credits for pointing this truth out after he read through the original manuscript of this book.

example, they recognize that God told Adam and Eve to fill, subdue, and take dominion of the Earth, but they wrongly think the power of those Words ended with the Fall of humanity. They think God's Words to Adam and Eve ceased producing when that dispensation ended.

In their compartmentalized way of thinking, dispensationalists mark the end of dispensations, and at each of those points they envision God enacting a new plan.

Christians with a progressive worldview see things differently. God's Word never fails and His plans never fail. Everything God spoke directly from His own mouth or anything "God spoke by the mouth of His holy prophets from ancient time" is already or will be fulfilled (Acts 3:21). Everything He ever has done is another step toward His ultimate goal of summing up all things in Jesus.

The Future Glory

The closer we get to the Second Coming of Jesus Christ, the more we will see the people of God transformed into His image and glory.

It will happen first within the Church. As God's glory increasingly manifests, Christians will be changed. Paul explained:

> *But we all, with unveiled face beholding as in a mirror the glory of the Lord, are being transformed into the same image from glory to glory, just as from the Lord, the Spirit.* (II Cor. 3:18)

As individuals within the Church mature, God's universal Church matures. As God's glory manifests in the corporate gathering, His people will be transformed progressively into His image and glory.

Then the day will come when Jesus Christ physically returns and we will see Him as He is. John writes:

> *We know that when He appears, we shall be like Him, because we shall see Him just as He is.* (I John 3:2b)

On that day, we shall be transformed fully. Any carnality remaining within us shall be dispelled. The nature of Jesus inside of us shall manifest fully. We shall become as He is.

Not only in holiness, but also our physical bodies will be transformed. Paul explained that our mortal, corrupt bodies will be metamorphosed into imperishable, glorified bodies (I Cor. 15:50-57). This will happen to Christians both living and dead. Those who are alive at our Lord's coming will be transformed. So also those who are in the graves will arise and be transformed. Paul wrote:

> ...we shall not all sleep, but we shall all
> be changed, in a moment, in the twin-
> kling of an eye, at the last trumpet; for the
> trumpet will sound, and the dead will be
> raised imperishable, and we shall be
> changed.   (I Cor. 15:51-52)

This is inevitable. God's children are "predestined to become conformed to the image of His Son" (Rom. 8:29). This is our destiny.

Jesus spoke of the glorious day, saying:

> "...an hour is coming, in which all who
> are in the tombs shall hear His voice, and
> shall come forth; those who did the good
> deeds to a resurrection of life, those who
> committed the evil deeds to a resurrection
> of judgment."   (John 5:28-29)

As the righteous are taken into the joy of God, the wicked shall be cast away from His presence eternally.

What then awaits God's people after they are glorified?

Jesus explained:

> *"Then the righteous will shine forth as the sun in the kingdom of their Father."*
> (Matt. 13:43)

Shining as the sun, God's children shall rule and reign with Him eternally.

The Progressive Worldview Showing the Glory Ahead

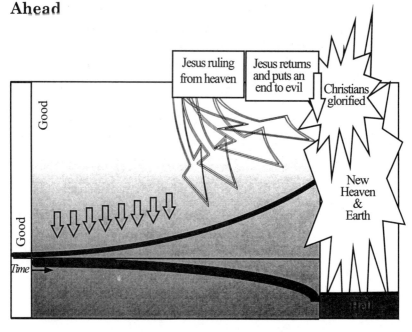

Once Christians have been glorified, then Creation itself will be brought into the glory belonging to the children of God. Paul explained that the whole of

Bringing the Future into Focus

Creation is longing for a day when it shall be liberated from corruption. That liberation shall happen after Christians come into their full inheritance as children of God (Rom. 8:19-22). God's children, with Jesus Christ, will bring a new order into Creation itself (Matt. 13:43). Corruption will be eliminated. Suffering, disease, and death will cease. Pain will be no more. The Earth shall bring forth an abundance. Jesus will exert His power and subject all things to Himself. Then He will rule and reign with His people over a new heaven and a new Earth.

 **The Future Hope**

Progressive Christians are filled with hope and optimism. They believe the Church is rising to maturity, the Kingdom and glory of God will fill the Earth, God will open the eyes of the Jews, and a worldwide revival is ahead of us. When Jesus returns for the final triumph, He will rid this created world of evil, transform His people, and create* a new heaven and a new Earth.

Dispensational Premillennialists have a different hope. They believe there will be a new heaven and Earth; however, they envision many catastrophic and terrible events before Jesus manifests His victory. Between now and then, they believe the world will get worse and worse. The hope on the forefront of their minds is that Jesus will soon come to *rapture* His people, that is, take them off of the Earth before He pours out His wrath upon this evil world.

This doctrine of an imminent *rapture* is so important and prominent in Dispensational Premillennial thinking that we need to address it.

The teaching of a rapture is developed by dispensationalists from a passage in I Thessalonians:

---

* Although we will not discuss it in this book, there is a debate among Christian teachers as to whether or not God will completely destroy this present Earth and then create a brand new one or if God simply will renew this present Earth.

Bringing the Future into Focus

> *For the Lord Himself will descend from heaven with a shout, with the voice of the archangel, and with the trumpet of God; and the dead in Christ shall rise first. Then we who are alive and remain shall be caught up together with them in the clouds to meet the Lord in the air, and thus we shall always be with the Lord.*
>
> (I Thes. 4:16-17)

In the above passage, we are told that those who are alive shall be "caught up," which in the Latin translation of the New Testament is the word, *raptura*, from which we get our modern-day word *rapture*.

Indeed, there will come a day in the future when Christians who are alive at the time of the return of Jesus Christ shall be caught up to meet the Lord in the air.

How and when this will happen is debated strongly among different Christian groups. As we explained earlier, Dispensational Premillennialists teach that the rapture will occur at the beginning of seven-year Tribulation (Pretrib rapture). Most Restorational Premillennialists say that the rapture will take place at the end of seven-year Tribulation (Postrib rapture).

The majority of the Church—historically and around the world today—disagrees with both of these views. In fact, most do not believe in a rapture as it is taught by dispensationalists and restorationalists.

To see the more commonly held belief, you first must change your focus away from the lifting of Christians off of the Earth and look at the major event, which is the return of Jesus. His appearance is the main event, not Christians floating into the air.

Envision Him appearing in the sky.

The Second Coming of Our Lord Jesus

Most of the Church around the world believe that when Jesus returns He will:

- Come with His angels
- Resurrect the dead to life
- Cause every knee to bow in His presence
- Judge the living and the dead
- Separate the tares from the wheat
- Transform Christians physically and spiritually into His image and glory
- Send the wicked to hell

It is important to realize that historically most of the Church have believed and taught that all of these events will take place at the Second Coming of Jesus Christ.

Bringing the Future into Focus

In contrast, Dispensational Premillennialists (and to a lesser extent, Restorational Premillennialists) divide up these events and see them occurring at several different points as shown in the diagram below.

The Dispensational View Showing the Consummation in Several Stages

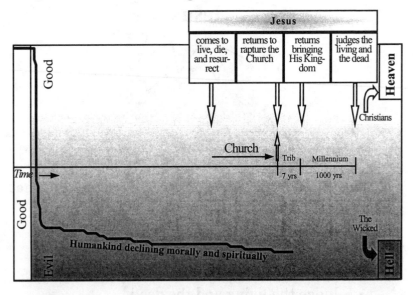

When we examine the Dispensational Premillennial view, we see that they believe Jesus will return not just once, but three times. Though most dispensationalists do not like to discuss this, it is a point of contention between them and the rest of the Church who believe in a Second Coming, but not a Third and Fourth Coming.

If we envision the Second Coming as one grand finale, the rapture of Christians becomes a much smaller part of this event. In fact, historically the Church has minimized this aspect of the Second Coming and focused directly on the appearance of Jesus in the sky and the ensuing final judgment.

The rapture is further minimized depending upon what Christians believe will happen after the appearance of Jesus Christ. Will we be taken to heaven or will we live on the new Earth? If we, His people, are to be lifted off of the Earth and then carried away to a distant place, then, indeed, the rapture is a significant event. In contrast, if Jesus is going to create a new Earth, bring New Jerusalem down to the new Earth, and then live with us *here* forever, then the rapture will be only a brief lifting of His people while He transforms this world.

We can compare this temporary lifting with how Noah's ark was lifted from the earth in the days of the flood. The ark was lifted by the rising water as God transformed the earth beneath, but then the ark settled back down to the earth.

It is this view which I hold as a Christian with a progressive view of Scripture. I believe Revelation 21 literally. There will be a new heaven and a new Earth, and then Jesus will usher the city called New Jerusalem down to the new Earth.

It is okay to call our future eternal dwelling place "heaven," but we must understand that this heaven is not some distant location where people will be floating in the sky. Rather heaven will come to Earth. We are not going away; He is returning.

Other Eschatological Views

It will be helpful at this point in our study to consider some of the other eschatological views held by various Christian groups. We have been developing the progressive view of endtime events and contrasting it to Dispensational and Restorational Premillennialism. As we mentioned in an earlier chapter, there are three other major eschatological views held by Christians: Historic Premillennialism, Amillennialism, and Postmillennialism. For the benefit of those readers who are interested in these views, I will take this chapter and the next to offer brief descriptions and make a few simple comparisons. Those who do not care to hear about these alternate eschatological views may skip this chapter and the next, and then continue with the book, beginning at chapter 33 where we again focus on the progressive worldview and its implications.

Historic Premillennialism simply refers to the view of a few Christian leaders in Church history who made reference in their writings to a hope of Jesus returning to Earth and setting up His Kingdom here for a 1,000-year Millennium. After the millennial reign, they envisioned Jesus judging all humanity, sending the wicked to hell, and taking the righteous to heaven.

Historic Premillennialism

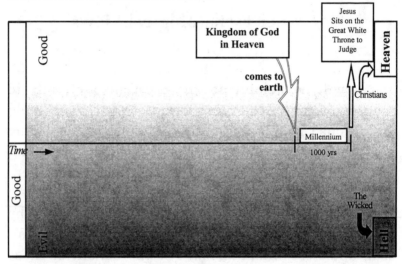

Christians who follow Dispensational and Restorational Premillennialism agree with Historic Premillennialism, but their beliefs are distinguished from it because dispensationalism and restorationalism are more fully developed worldviews offering complete scenarios of how events have and will continue to unfold. Further, the dispensational and restorational worldviews are relatively new, that is, developed within the last 150 years. Today we have no way of knowing whether the leaders in history who believed in Historic Premillennialism would have embraced the details proposed by modern Dispensational or Restorational Premillennialists.

With Historic Premillennialism being a clear-cut, simple-to-understand view, some Christian teachers today claim allegiance to it. They hold to the hope of a future 1,000-year reign of Jesus on the Earth, yet they refrain from committing themselves to the additional details offered by dispensationalists or restorationalists.

Our next eschatological view is Amillennialism. This has been and continues to be the most widely held eschatological view in the Church worldwide. Augustine (354-430 AD) is accredited with developing this view during the Fourth Century. Since then, most of the Church has embraced it, and most of the influential leaders in Church history, such as Martin Luther and John Calvin, taught it. Today most historic, mainline denominations (non-evangelical), along with some evangelical church groups, hold this view.

Amillennialism builds on the same four great works which Reformed Theology emphasizes: Creation, the Fall, Redemption, and the Consummation. From there it teaches that the Kingdom of God was established when Jesus sat down on His throne 2,000 years ago. Jesus has been and continues to rule over the Earth through the Church. The Church will continue to exist as God's representative in the Earth, while the rest of the world continues on a moral and spiritual decline. Just before the end, Satan's activity will increase greatly, but then Jesus will return to rescue the Church out of an evil world.

Amillennialists do not believe there will be a 1,000-year period in the future when the Kingdom of God comes to Earth. Rather, they teach that the millennial reign of Jesus began 2,000 years ago. This is where they get the name "Amillennial" ("a" from the Latin prefix meaning "no" and millennium meaning

Bringing the Future into Focus

1,000; hence, giving us "no 1,000-year reign"). Amillennialists teach that the Church has been in the reign of Jesus since He sat down on His throne. We will continue to be in this Kingdom reign until Jesus returns to put an end to evil, judge the world, and send people to heaven or hell.

Amillennial Eschatology

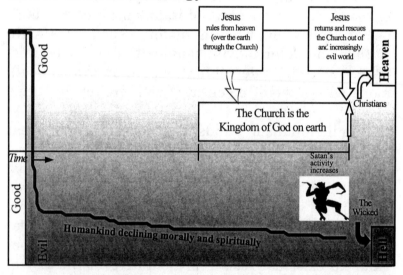

Christians with a progressive understanding agree with the Amillennialists that the Kingdom began 2,000 years ago; however, they object to several other Amillennial points, one being the Amillennial tendency to equate the Church with the Kingdom of God on Earth. This leads to several misconceptions which have significant implications.

Consider the Crusades of the Eleventh through Thirteenth Centuries. During that period the established Church thought of herself as the Kingdom of

God on Earth. With this thinking, Church leaders encouraged and commissioned people to free Jerusalem from enemy control, conquer the Muslims, and use force to compel all people to enter the Kingdom of God. Thousands of Christians and Muslim people died.

Today it is easy to see the erroneous reasoning behind the Crusades. If the Church is seen as the Kingdom on Earth, then it may become a warring, violent entity. On the other hand, if the Church is the Temple of God, destined for the glory of God, then She must have a corresponding focus.

Even today, Christians who confuse the two tend to make the Church into a warring, conquering entity, rather than a glorious, holy Temple for the presence of God.

To see the Kingdom and the Church as two distinct entities, as progressive Christians do, envision a natural kingdom as it would have existed in Bible days. Within a kingdom was a temple, that is, a specific location where people could worship their god. The kingdom was much bigger than the temple; it surrounded the temple, and it extended throughout all the regions under the king's authority. In an analogous fashion, the Church is the Temple which God is building for Himself. The Kingdom of God encompasses the Church but it also reaches far beyond it.

Progressive Christians say that the Church has the keys of the Kingdom in the sense that She can release the will of the King into the Earth. She can direct and teach people to govern their lives in submission to the King. Through Her inspiration, people may move into the power of God. With the blessings of the Church, people can rise and be victorious in business, government, technology, education, art, and every other area of society.

Since Amillennialists equate the Church with the Kingdom of God on Earth, they tend to think of God's will only being established within the walls of the Church. They greatly honor the Church, but they tend to think of it as a monolithic ark moving through time within a big evil world. Hence, they do not have much hope for good happening outside of the Church. (A proponent of Amillennialism would say that I am being too harsh; please understand that I am making this point in contrast to the progressive worldview.)

Amillennialists see society as being on a spiritual downward slide. They teach that just before the end of the world, Satan's activity will increase greatly. An apostasy then will come over the Earth. Finally in the end, Jesus will return to rescue the Church from out of an increasingly evil world.

This identifies another key distinction between Amillennialism and the progressive worldview... progressive Christians have a much more optimistic view of the future.

 **Postmillennial Eschatology**

Postmillennialism is another eschatological view which thousands of Christians hold today. I will describe it and then show how this view compares with the endtime events of the progressive worldview.

Building on the four foundations of Reformed Theology (Creation, the Fall, Redemption, and Consummation), Postmillennialism teaches that the Church will continue to grow until it attains a victorious position in the Earth, establishing peace and prosperity for humankind. Jesus will return to Earth after that victorious reign. Hence, the name "Postmillennial" indicating that Jesus will return "post" the Millennium.

Basic Postmillennial Eschatology

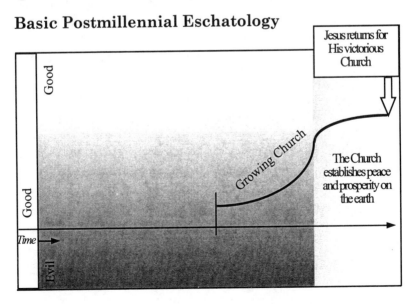

Good

Good

Jesus returns for His victorious Church

The Church establishes peace and prosperity on the earth

Growing Church

Time

Evil

Bringing the Future into Focus

This Postmillennial understanding became commonly accepted during the late 1700's among Evangelical Christians throughout America and parts of Europe. Leaders, such as Jonathan Edwards, who is the most known preacher of the Great Awakening (1740-1780), were strong proponents of this view. Also the Puritans in both England and America aggressively promoted Postmillennialism. It eventually grew to dominate American Protestant Christianity during the 1800's.

Postmillennial eschatology was displaced in America by Premillennialism during the 1900's. However, in recent years, especially since the year 2,000, Postmillennialism has been revived. Much of this is due to an increase of books teaching this position, but also many Christians have become disillusioned with Dispensational Premillennialism and its repeated mispredictions of endtime events and the return of Jesus. With a whole new millennium ahead of us, many Christians are looking to the future with long-range goals and optimistic hopes.

Modern Postmillennialists divide themselves into two groups: "Partial Preterists" and "Full Preterists." This distinction is based on how much of the Book of Revelation and Matthew, chapter 24, they believe already has been fulfilled. Rather than take the time to further discuss this distinction, I refer you the recommended books listed in the Appendix.

All Postmillennialists believe that the tribulation described in Matthew 24:5-21 occurred between 50 and 70 AD when Jerusalem was destroyed. Hence, there will be no Great Tribulation in the future before Jesus returns.

160

Postmillennial eschatology promises a very optimistic future. The Church will arise to glory and the Kingdom of God will advance progressively until it fills the Earth. Unlike Amillennialism and Premillennialism, the Postmillennial view does not envision a great apostasy coming over the Earth in the future. It does not see Jesus returning to rescue the Church out of an increasingly evil world. On the contrary, it sees the Church manifesting the Kingdom of God and actually changing the world into a better place. Jesus will return for a victorious Church.

Christians with a progressive worldview are optimists, but not quite as optimistic as Postmillennialists. As we have explained, the progressive worldview envisions the Church continually advancing, but there will be a struggle between righteousness and unrighteousness until the return of our Lord.

Furthermore, we must not equate the progressive worldview with Postmillennialism, because Jesus will not return "post" the Millennium. Rather, He will return when the Father releases Him. It shall not be at the end of the reign of the Kingdom of God, but His return will be another step in establishing His reign. Hence, "Postmillennial" would be a misnomer if applied to the progressive worldview.

Another reason we should distinguish Progressive thinking from Postmillennialism is because various Postmillennial proponents today are so divergent in their teachings. Many Postmillennialists embrace Replacement Theology (Christians have replaced the Jews as far as the promises of God). Others make the mistake of equating the Church with the Kingdom of

God. Some Postmillennialists are Reconstructionists (teaching that we should restructure the world's governments using the Old Testament laws as our pattern). Other Postmillennialists teach that God is restoring Creation back to the conditions of the Garden of Eden (rather than progressively working out His plan which will turn Creation into a much more glorious place than it was in the beginning). Numerous books give these and other variations on the basic Postmillennial view. I will not take the time to repeat nor explain all those variations. My point is a word of caution that modern Postmillennialism encompasses varied positions on the actual outworkings of endtime events.

At this point, let's recognize that the progressive worldview shares much, but not all, of the optimism of the Postmillennial view.

Abandoning Premillennialism

The progressive worldview leads a person to believe the following points which are important for our eschatology:

1. The Church will arise to glory, unity, power, and maturity before the return of Jesus.

2. The Kingdom of God was established over heaven and Earth 2,000 years ago, and the Kingdom will advance progressively until it fills the Earth.

3. The manifest presence of God will increase within the Church and flow out to fill the Earth.

4. The Jews will be made one with Christians before Jesus returns.

5. A worldwide revival is inevitable, and Christianity will become the most dominant force on Earth.

6. At His Second Coming, Jesus will judge humanity, remove evil from the world, and bring all things into submission to Himself.

Each of these statements are incompatible with the eschatology of Dispensational Premillennialism. Therefore, if we recognize the progressive worldview as accurate biblically, then we must reject Pretribulational Premillennialism.

Bringing the Future into Focus

It is not easy for a dispensationalist to abandon the compartmentalized way of thinking. Those thought patterns can be rooted so deeply that it is difficult to see Scriptures in any other light.

This is perhaps most obvious when it comes to their belief in a future Millennium. The problem is not only that they see the Millennium as a distinct block of time with a beginning and an end, but they also categorize certain Old Testament passages to fit before the Millennium, while others are fitted within the Millennium. In particular, Bible passages that describe the people of God struggling and getting beaten by the devil are placed before the Millennium. On the other hand, passages which show the Church victorious and reigning on Earth automatically are moved into their picture of the future Millennium.

Progressive Christianity does not have this fixation.

Consider Isaiah 60:2:

> *"For behold, darkness will cover the*
> *earth,*
> *And deep darkness the peoples;*
> *But the Lord will rise upon you,*
> *And His glory will appear upon you."*

Earlier we discussed this and saw how restorationalists like to quote this passage. In particular, they like to portray the Church rising in glory in the midst of the world becoming darker. They see hope for the Church, but not for the world.

For the dispensationalists studying this verse, the darkness over the world stands out. They don't see the glory coming upon the Church until the Millennium starts.

Think about this verse through the progressive worldview. This Bible passage is not necessarily saying that deep darkness will be a future reality. It is stating a fact that, indeed, there will be dark times in this world. However, the main point of this passage is the positive hope that God's glory will come upon His people. What will be the consequence? The very next verse tells us:

> "And nations will come to your light,
> And kings to the brightness of your
> rising." (Is. 60:3)

Isaiah goes on to tell of glorious days for God's people when the nations will respond to the glory of God, serve the people of God, and bring their wealth for the service of God (Is. 60:3-22).

The point is that the world will not stay in the deep darkness to which is referred in Isaiah 60:2. The increasing light and glory of God will change the darkness. The Church is a light to the world, a city set on a hill. Nations will respond!

I could go on to show how other verses are interpreted, but the point already has been made—we each interpret Scriptures through the worldview we already have embraced.

I suggest we embrace the understanding of the Kingdom which Jesus gave us, that the Kingdom grows as seeds. This is the progressive worldview.

Apply it to our understanding of the Millennium. Will it be a literal 1,000-year block of time starting at some point in the future? Or is the Kingdom as a seed growing into the biggest tree?

In order to address this question, we need to examine the Scriptures from which we obtain our understanding of the Millennium. There is only one chapter in the Bible which mentions the 1,000-year reign. It is Revelation 20. The Millennium is mentioned several times in that chapter, two of which are in the passage below:

> *And I saw an angel coming down from heaven, having the key of the abyss and a great chain in his hand. And he laid hold of the dragon, the serpent of old, who is the devil and Satan, and bound him for a thousand years, and threw him into the abyss,...until the thousand years were completed....* (Rev. 20:1-3)

If we take this passage literally, then we conclude that this Kingdom reign will be a literal 1,000 years in length, beginning at some point in the future.

However, there is another way to understand this 1,000-year reign.

Most of the Church around the world (Amillennialists and Postmillennialists) will point out that the Jewish people often used specific numbers to refer to principles. For example, when the number 1,000 is used elsewhere in Scripture, it does not refer to a literal number, but rather to a "fullness." Consider how we are told that God owns "the cattle on a thousand hills" (Ps. 50:10). This does not mean God owns the cattle only on 1,000 hills, but rather that He owns the cattle on all hills. Similarly, we can read how Moses blessed the people that God would increase them a thousand-fold (Deut. 1:11), and God's love is described as reaching to a thousand generations, not necessarily referring to a literal number, but to the full reach of His glorious love (Ex. 20:6). For similar uses of 1,000, see Psalms 68:17; 84:10; and 90:4.

With this understanding, Amillennial and Post-millennial Christians will say that Jesus reigns for a 1,000 years, not referring to a literal length of time, but to a fullness of times. They also will say that His reign began 2,000 years ago.

This understanding can be shocking to Premillennial Christians who never have heard it before. They may raise the accusation that the Scriptures are being "spiritualized." In reality, if we take the number 1,000 and say that it only can be taken literally, then we are guilty of "Westernizing" the Scriptures, that is, taking the Jewish style of communication and forcing it into our Western language structure.

It is important to note that most of the Church throughout history and most Bible scholars in the world today do not take the 1,000-year reference to mean a literal 1,000 years. Historically, we know that great leaders such as Augustine, Martin Luther, and John Calvin all taught that the Millennium was symbolic of the fullness of Jesus reigning through the Church. The Premillennial view did surface in small groups from time to time in history (Historic Premillennialism) and a few historic Church leaders did hold to Premillennialism. However, the vast majority of

Bringing the Future into Focus

Bible scholars gave it little or no credence. For example, John Calvin wrote very critically of Chiliasm, which is another name for the Premillennial view:

> But a little later there followed chiliasts, who limited the reign of Christ to a thousand years. Now their fiction is too childish either to need or to be worth a refutation.*

I have to agree with John Calvin and the vast majority of other Church leaders. A serious consideration of how the Jewish people communicated leads us to understand that the reign of Jesus is for a fullness of times. I would reconsider this if there were any other passages in the Bible which tell us that the reign of Jesus on Earth will be limited to a 1,000 years, but the *only* reference is in chapter 20 of Revelation, which is a very prophetic, visionary book, using other symbolic numbers (i.e., seven Spirits of God, the mark of 666, and 144,000 faithful ones). Furthermore, we have numerous other Bible passages which tell us that the Kingdom of God is an eternal Kingdom having no end (i.e., I Chron. 17:14; Is. 9:7; Dan. 2:44).

I believe the Kingdom of God was established over heaven and Earth 2,000 years ago and Jesus will reign forever.

---

* John T. McNeil, ed. John Calvin, *Institutes of the Christian Religion,* vol. 2 (Philadelphia: Westminster, 1960): 995.

34 The Revelation of Victory

In the Body of Christ today we can find hundreds of different ways in which the Book of Revelation has been interpreted. I do not claim to have all the answers. In fact, I still am mystified by many elements within the book. I cannot offer you a detailed explanation, but I can eliminate a few misconceptions.

In popular Evangelical Christianity today there has been story after story told about the coming Antichrist and the future evils to come. Those stories have been so emblazoned upon the minds of Christians that often they no longer can separate biblical fact from fiction.

For example, did you know that the Antichrist is never mentioned in the Book of Revelation? That fact can be shocking to some Christians. Many have developed the idea that the main message of Revelation is the coming rise of the Antichrist. Yet it is true—the word Antichrist never is mentioned in the Book of Revelation, not even once.

The Harlot and Beast are mentioned, and I could teach on that, but, instead, I will offer you a quick overview of the last book of the Bible.

Chapters one through four give an introduction, followed by seven letters to seven churches. We know historically that those churches actually existed in the time period when John wrote the Book of Revelation.

Bringing the Future into Focus

There are many truths in those letters which can be applied to any group of Christians in any time period; however, I believe that those letters originally were written to seven literal churches.

Beginning in chapter four of Revelation, John saw into heaven. The outstanding feature of his vision was Jesus ruling from His throne. John actually was seeing what was taking place in heaven 2,000 years ago after Jesus sat down at the right hand of the Father.

Once Jesus sat down on His throne, He began to unfold the plan of God. From chapter six to chapter 19, we see the exertion of our Lord's power and the expansion of His Kingdom over the entire Earth. We see the war in the heavenlies, that is, in the spiritual realm. I understand the Harlot and the Beast are spiritual entities, rather than natural beings. Of course, they have a negative influence upon humanity. Further, they seem to have some influence within the realm of government and religion. They fight against God, and those battles have profound and immediate implications for all people on Earth.

However, the main point is that they—and all of God's enemies—are conquered by our Lord Jesus. They are defeated in the spiritual realm, hence, freeing humanity. This the message of the Book of Revelation. It is not a book about the rise of evil. On the contrary, it is a book of our Lord's victory.

I will leave the details of interpretation to you and those who already have written numerous books on the subject. In order to expand your thinking, I can recommend the titles listed in the Appendix.

The Book of Revelation places the capstone of victory on our progressive worldview. Jesus is seated on His throne (Rev. 4). He reigns until every enemy is put under His feet (Rev. 4-20). The kingdoms of this world become the Kingdoms of our God (Rev. 11:15). The purified and glorious Church presents Herself to Jesus, ready for the Marriage Supper of the Lamb (Rev. 19). Satan is defeated and cast into the Lake of Fire (Rev. 20). Evil is eliminated and cast completely out of this realm (Rev. 20). A new heaven and Earth are created and God's people live with Him forever (Rev. 21-21).

Eschatology of the Progressive Worldview

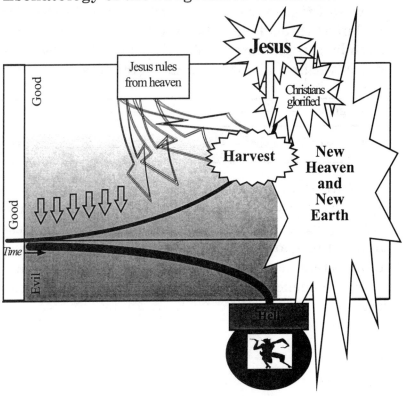

Bringing the Future into Focus

Having this progressive worldview, what shall I call my eschatology? Am I a Premillennialist, Amillennialist, or Postmillennialist? I agree with the Amillennialists that the Kingdom of God began 2,000 years ago. I also agree with the Premillennialists and the Postmillennialists that there will be a fuller manifestation of the Kingdom of God on Earth in the future. There are some aspects of each of these views which fit the progressive understanding of Scripture and some which do not. Because I have accepted the progressive worldview as the most biblically accurate worldview, I must claim a separate eschatological view—a Progressive Eschatology. That eschatology is explained throughout this book but it can be summarized by this statement: "The Kingdom of God is here, it is advancing, and it will come in fullness."

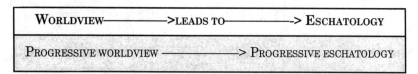

WORLDVIEW————————>LEADS TO————————-> ESCHATOLOGY

PROGRESSIVE WORLDVIEW ———————-> PROGRESSIVE ESCHATOLOGY

With this progressive worldview and progressive eschatology, I will take the rest of this book to discuss the implications of this understanding. Since these implications are in greatest variance to Dispensational Premillennialism (the most vocal view of American Evangelicals today), I will contrast these two views.

35 The Great Commission Hope

The progressive worldview and eschatology teach that Christians will fulfill the Great Commission.

Dispensational Premillennialism teaches that Christians will *not* fulfill the Great Commission.

After Jesus rose from the dead, He said:

> *"All authority has been given to Me in heaven and on earth. Go therefore and make disciples of all the nations...."*
>
> (Matt. 28:19)

Dispensationalists misinterpret these words to mean that we merely are to go and preach the Gospel to all people. In reality, Jesus commissioned His followers to do much more than that. He told them to "make disciples of all nations."

The impact of our Lord's Words can be grasped only if we put ourselves in the place of the disciples to whom He first was talking. It is analogous to a natural king who had been given authority over an empire and then told his ambassadors and soldiers to establish his authority throughout the empire. In this sense, Jesus is Lord. He will reign until every enemy is put under His feet (I Cor. 15:25). Jesus did not tell His followers simply to preach the Gospel, nor merely make a few disciples in a few nations, but actually to make the nations disciples of His. Furthermore, they should expect to succeed, because all authority now belongs to Jesus.

This is a hope promised several times in Scripture. The Psalm writers say:

> *All the ends of the earth will remember*
>   *and turn to the Lord,*
> *And all the families of the nations will*
>   *worship before Thee.*   (Ps. 22:27)

> *All nations whom Thou hast made shall*
>   *come and worship before Thee, O*
>   *Lord;*
> *And they shall glorify Thy name.*
>   (Ps. 86:9)

> *So the nations will fear the name of the*
>   *Lord,*
> *And all the kings of the earth Thy glory.*
>   (Ps. 102:15)

Christians with a progressive worldview believe this will happen. They see the Great Commission analogous to God's Words to Adam and Eve to multiply, fill, and subdue the Earth. Neither God's Words in the beginning nor Jesus' Words after His resurrection will fail. They are being fulfilled.

In contrast, dispensational Christians believe that we will preach the Gospel to every people group on Earth; however, most people will reject the message, and many of those who do believe eventually will turn away. Just as they believe God's Words to multiply, fill, and subdue have failed, so also they believe Jesus' Words to the disciples are merely a command which Christians will fail to fulfill. Of course, they believe that God will impose His Kingdom on Earth forcefully at the start of a future Millennium; however, according to dispensationalists, that forced victory will happen only after the Church has failed and Satan almost completely has taken over this world.

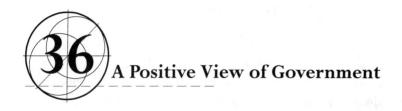

36 A Positive View of Government

Christians with a progressive worldview believe that God is taking over the governments of the world.

Dispensational Premillennialists believe that Satan is taking over the governments of this world.

This distinction has a profound impact on how Christians see and relate to their own political leaders and government as a whole.

Dispensationalists are constantly on the alert and suspicious of what their government is doing. They live with an us-versus-them mindset. They (except for a minority activist portion) invest little time and energy in trying to change their government, and what little they do, they engage in with a defeatist attitude.

Dispensationalists who fully have bought into the modern Pretribulational Premillennial view live in fear of their government, believing that soon the beast of the Book of Revelation will be manifesting in the political leaders of the world. They believe that one day their government will be taken over completely by the Antichrist, and will become the major force behind the killing of most Christians remaining on Earth.

Tragically, it is dispensational Christians in America who have fallen for this myth more than any other people. Many of them are convinced that their own nation was founded by deceived leaders with the goal of establishing Satan's kingdom on the Earth.

Bringing the Future into Focus

In the eyes of the larger Body of Christ (not to mention the non-Christian world) dispensationalists are viewed as paranoid isolationists. They are seen as people constantly feeding their own fears and not in touch with what truly is going on in society.

Christians with a progressive worldview have a very different understanding of government, leading them to a different outlook and lifestyle.

The progressive Christian's view matches Paul's words that government is a "minister of God" in the Earth (Rom. 13:4). Of course, there are some evil individuals holding positions of authority, but the overall concept of government is God's hand reaching into the Earth to establish peace and order. Government is basically good.

In stark contrast, dispensationalists think of government as a necessary evil, becoming ever more evil and soon to be destroyed by God.

Christians with a progressive worldview believe that government not only basically is good, but an eternal good. Rather than destroying government, God is in the process of taking over the governments of this world and setting up His eternal Kingdom government which shall have no end.

Progressive Christians have hope where dispensationalists have fear.

This distinction is very evident in Christians' view of the United Nations. Most dispensationalists are suspicious—if not fully convinced—that the United Nations is the instrument of Satan which shall someday unite the world's governments to set up Satan's kingdom and kill Christians throughout the Earth.

In contrast, the progressive Christian believes that:

> *...there is no authority except from God, and those which exist are established by God.* (Rom. 13:1)

God is the One who established the United Nations—not Satan. Of course, this or any form of government may do specific acts contrary to the will of God; however, God progressively will establish His will in the Earth using every form of government.

The progressive Christian has great hope for worldwide and local government. Back when God spoke the original blessing, He destined many positive things to happen. Humankind will fill and subdue the Earth. One of the implications of this is that humanity will establish a greater level of peace in the Earth.

This idea of future peace can be shocking to dispensational Christians because it is diametrically opposed to their belief system. They believe the warnings of Matthew 24:6-7 are still ahead of us, and therefore, wars, violence, and hatred will increase.

In contrast, the Christian with a progressive worldview accepts coming peace as inevitable from many Scriptural perspectives. Of course, there will be many battles between righteousness and unrighteousness ahead, but the overall direction in which humankind is moving is toward dominion. Jesus has authority over heaven and Earth. He will continue to reign until all enemies will be put under His feet; the kingdoms of the world are becoming the Kingdoms of our God and the knowledge of the glory of the Lord will cover the Earth. Of course, perfect peace will not be established until Jesus actually returns; however, the Christian who understands the Scriptures progressively sees the Kingdom of God growing as a seed and the will of God progressively filling the Earth.

# A Positive View of Society

Dispensational Premillennialists hold a fundamental belief that people are evil and getting worse.

Progressive Christians have a much more positive
view of society and humankind.

This distinction has profound implications for the
everyday Christian. Dispensationalists are looking for
society to slide downward morally and spiritually.
They see the Church as the only positive thing in the
Earth, an ark floating in a flood of evil. The world is
seen as something which must be conquered and done
away with, and soon God will pour out His wrath upon
humanity.

Seeing the world through such negative eyes, dispensationalists listen for bad news. Whenever the
news media reports war breaking out somewhere in
the world, children in schools killing other children, or
violence in some other form, dispensationalists interpret the events as confirmation of their own beliefs
concerning society's increasing corruption. Whenever
there is a report of an earthquake in some part of the
world, a downturn in the economy, or a famine, they
take it as a sign that God is threatening to pour out
His wrath.

In contrast, the progressive Christian listens to
bad news reports, recognizing the resulting pain and
heartbreak, yet confident that all things ultimately

are being turned for God's glory. Negative events are tragic; however, they merely are short-term downturns in the overall positive direction the Earth is headed.

The truth is that the progressive Christian holds a much more long-range, accurate view of history, knowing that society has had thousands of years of ups and downs, many generations showing terrible evil and moral corruption worse than the present. As we discussed earlier, in the days of Noah the entire population of the world, except Noah, had thoughts which were only evil continually. Throughout the Old Testament we learn of most cultures outside of the Jewish nation worshipping false gods, such as Baal, wooden statues, and the dead. When God destroyed Sodom and Gomorrah, He could not find ten righteous men. (I have traveled the world, and I do not believe there is any city on Earth in which we could not find ten devout and sincere Christians.)

In secular history we see an ancient world lost in darkness. Many societies engaged in human sacrifice and cannibalism. Here in the Americas, the Aztecs were offering human sacrifices by the thousands. Up until the last hundred years, slavery and genocidal wars have been common among people groups scattered around the world. During the Roman Empire, thousands of people gathered in coliseums to watch the slaughter of Christians and others. Historians report that in Europe during the Middle Ages crime was much greater than it is in our times.

When Christians today listen to their daily news, it is easy to lose sight of the fact that Christianity is the largest religion among the six billion people of the world. While television can bring home a tragic incident from anywhere in the world, it is easy to forget that billions of people are living in peace, working their jobs, and raising families. When Christians hear of some new law contrary to their standards and ethics, they quickly forget that Christianity is growing more rapidly today than at any time in history.

Dispensationalism especially feeds on the negative sensationalism which easily over-shadows the good. Not only do televangelists use catastrophic messages to urge people to act, but the Pretribulational Premillennial view promotes a basic assumption that everything is getting worse.

Dispensationalists may labor to benefit society, but inside they nurture a belief that our country and world are disintegrating. They may pray, "God, save our country," but in their hearts they hold an unshakable belief that God will not answer.

The progressive Christian sees no such inescapable downward slide and, in fact, believes that humanity is able to repent and turn to God at any time. Furthermore, the overall road throughout the ages is positive. Of course, there are still many problems in the Earth and much work to be done. However, the progressive Christian knows God confidently is advancing His will throughout the Earth. Not only will the Church arise, but Christians will continue to promote truth and righteousness in every area of society. Indeed, there will be numerous battles. However, the advancement of God's will in the Earth is inevitable.

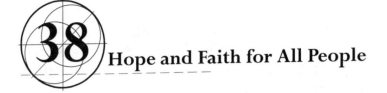

38 Hope and Faith for All People

Not only do dispensationalists view society as a whole as going downhill, but they also cultivate negative attitudes toward specific people groups.

In contrast, progressive Christianity has hope for all people.

We already have discussed how dispensationalists view government with suspicion, but there are more groups than government under their watchful eyes.

Dispensationalists maintain a distance and mistrust of Arabs and other Islamic people. This is primarily based on their belief that Jews are God's covenant people, in the sense that they will receive special favor, being restored as a nation and raised to rule over the Earth. In contrast, the progressive view sees Jews as God's covenant people, in the sense that they will receive special favor, being made one with the Body of Christ. The dispensational belief leads Christians to oppose any group who comes against Israel as a nation. Since many Arabs oppose Israel as a nation, dispensationalists tend to think of them as the enemies of God.

In contrast, progressive Christianity has a more positive view of these people. As we discussed earlier, all people will be swept into the worldwide revival preceding the return of our Lord Jesus.

Bringing the Future into Focus

Dispensationalists believe that almost the whole world will come against the Jews during the latter part of the Tribulation. In particular, they teach that countries referred to in the Bible as Gog and Magog will raise armies to destroy the Holy Land. Most dispensationalists today interpret Gog and Magog to be Russia and China. I do not want to accuse dispensationalists of being unloving, but anyone involved in Premillennial eschatology will cultivate a suspicion that Russia and China could turn against Christians and Jews any time.

This is no small issue. Dispensational authors who write endtime books repeatedly insert negative comments about both of these countries. The person unaware of this tendency may not even notice it; however, even a casual reading by someone looking for this will see it as very evident.

Dispensational Premillennialists also believe that Satan is and will continue taking control of a world-wide religious system. With this mindset they tend to be very suspicious of any religious group—Christian or non-Christian—which promotes and works for unity on a large scale. Ecumenical movements are mistrusted. Even the "Organized Church," in contrast to independent, locally-run congregations, are held in strong suspicion. Although the more scholarly Premillennialists would not abandon themselves to such fears, tens of thousands of followers of popular Premillennialism already have. Many mistrust any Christian group which is not also Premillennial in its beliefs, since they are convinced that anyone not firmly holding up their defenses against an ever-increasingly-evil world will themselves soon be deceived.

In contrast, a Christian with a progressive worldview is looking for increasing unity in the Body of Christ. He or she wants Christians in different denominations to become united in faith and doctrine. Of course, some of today's ecumenical movements insist on compromises that a Bible-believing Christian cannot embrace, yet, progressive Christians are confidently looking for a true, Holy-Spirit-inspired unity of the Church across the world. We will experience the answer to the prayer of our Lord: that we will be made one (John 17:20-23).

Dispensationalists have no room for such unity to come before the return of Jesus Christ. Their worldview demands division and mistrust.

They have an especially strong mistrust of Roman Catholics. Some of their suspicions stem from their fears of the Harlot of Revelation arising, but the fears of the more studious dispensationalists are founded in a specific interpretation of Daniel, chapter two.

Daniel interpreted a dream for King Nebuchadnezzar. Earlier we discussed this dream and saw a statue made of four parts, but then a rock came, crushed the statue, then grew into a mountain, and finally filled the whole Earth. Daniel interpreted the dream saying that there would be four kingdoms ruling over the world. We know historically there have been four kingdoms: the Babylonian kingdom, the Medo-Persian kingdom, the Greek Empire, and then the Roman Empire. The significant point for our discussion has to do with God's promise that He would send His *Rock* to crush all of these kingdoms, and then set up His eternal Kingdom in the midst of the fourth kingdom—the Roman Empire.

Dispensational and progressive Christians agree concerning the above understanding of Daniel, chapter two, however they disagree as to what the Roman kingdom is.

Progressive Christians teach, as does most of the Body of Christ, that 2,000 years ago Jesus came to the Earth and set up His Kingdom—that was during the time when the Roman Empire was ruling.

In contrast, dispensationalists believe God's Kingdom will come to the Earth at some point in the future. Therefore, if they are going to fit Daniel, chapter two, into their understanding, they must envision some type of Roman kingdom ruling over the Earth when that future *Rock* comes to Earth. Furthermore, they must envision God crushing that Roman kingdom in order to establish His Kingdom on Earth.

Dispensational Premillennialists *need* an evil Roman empire to fit their scenario of endtime events. Not all dispensationalists will label the present Roman Catholic Church as this evil entity, but it is a reoccurring theme and a constant suspicion.

Some dispensationalists suggest that there will be a literal government which shall arise: "Revived Roman Empire." However, that idea is difficult for most dispensationalists to hold because they also believe in the imminent return of Jesus. To be consistent they must locate some Roman ruling entity on the Earth right now which God could crush at any moment.

Although most dispensational teachers will not come out and label the Roman Catholic Church as this evil entity, this thought underlies and repeatedly resurfaces in Premillennial eschatology.

If not Roman Catholics, then perhaps the commonwealth of nations in Europe. Dispensationalists often suggest that this is the evil government which God shall soon destroy.

So grounded in fear and prejudice is the dispensational system of thought that followers must keep firm walls erected in their hearts against numerous peoples of the world. Governments always will be held in suspicion. Ecumenical movements are futile or even demonic endeavors. Roman Catholics are definitely the enemy. Whenever some evil is carried out by individuals associated with the Islamic faith—such as terrorist activity—dispensational Christians reinforce their prejudice of Arabic people, which their worldview dictates.

Throughout the last 100 years, various groups have spent time under the most severe judgments that dispensationalists can raise—that the associated leaders are the Antichrist himself. The leaders of Germany, Italy, Japan, Russia, China, and Iraq each have been labeled Satan's own instrument.

While the eyes of dispensational Christians wander the Earth looking for those under the influence of the Antichrist, progressive Christians are looking for all to come under the influence of *The Christ*.

God has a heart and plan for all people. Rather than pour out His wrath upon humanity, God is about to pour out His Spirit on the entire world. Through

Bringing the Future into Focus

Abraham, *all* the families of the Earth will be blessed. The world is not going to turn against Christians and Jews in the future. Rather, the world will turn toward God with Christians and Jews. A worldwide revival is inevitable. This will include governments, Arabs, traditional Churches (including Roman Catholics), the commonwealth of Europe, America, China, Russia, Japan, Iraq, Israel, and, indeed, the whole world.

Optimistic Care of the Earth

Dispensational Premillennialists believe that God will soon pour out His wrath upon the Earth.

Progressive Christians believe that the Earth is being redeemed progressively and it, along with the heavens, soon will be transformed into a new heaven and Earth.

Dispensationalists have an unshakable belief in a coming Great Tribulation, when the judgments described in the Book of Revelation will be released upon the Earth. God will send famines and earthquakes, kill the vast majority of humanity, burn up the Earth's plant life, and completely destroy the environment.

Progressive Christians will point out that this belief of dispensationalists' is in direct contradiction to the covenant God established with Noah. As we noted earlier, God promised:

> *"I will never again curse the ground on account of man...."* (Gen. 8:21)

Dispensationalists do not believe this. They envision God soon devastating the Earth.

In contrast, Christians with a progressive worldview believe God will keep all of His covenants. Again let me say that this is the very foundation of the progressive worldview.

Bringing the Future into Focus

Furthermore, progressive Christians see God actively redeeming Creation. They do not envision a coming seven-year period of destruction. Quite to the contrary, they believe it is God's desire for people to care for the Earth.

As we explained earlier, the promise of subduing of the Earth is not in the sense of conquering nor exploiting. We can see God's original intentions as we study His commission and blessing upon Adam and Eve. Immediately after blessing them, God put them in the Garden of Eden to care for it. In that context, God wants humankind to care for the Earth, managing things so that the Earth will be fruitful, abundant, and beautiful.

God also blessed humankind with the ability to progress—to build cities, construct homes, engineer bridges, invent tools, develop ideas, make technological advancements, improving life for everyone. Many Christians miss this part of God's blessing because they think that if God's will actually were realized on the Earth, it would all be one Garden of Eden. That, however, is not accurate. God intended for humanity to advance in the midst of the Garden.

The most obvious proof of this is to glance ahead to the end of the Book of Revelation. Heaven is not a garden. It is a city—Jerusalem. Jesus is building mansions for us, not mud huts. Not only are there dirt paths amidst the flowers, but there are also streets paved with gold. God's idea of utopia—the ultimate goal of dominion—would not be just a Garden of Eden over the whole Earth. It would be humankind subduing and ruling over the Earth so that the Earth would serve all fully and perfectly.

Now in saying all of this, I am not implying that humankind will attain this goal without the intervention of God. What I am describing is the direction of dominion. I am identifying the force pushing humankind ahead. It originated with God's original blessing and it is active upon all people.

Of course, we know that Adam and Eve sinned. People continue to rebel against God's will. Yet, people's failures cannot supercede God's spoken Word. Ultimately, the will of God shall be established. No demon, no human, no obstacle can stand in the way of the ultimate fulfillment of what He has spoken Not one jot or tittle will pass away until all has been fulfilled (Matt. 5:18).

This understanding leads the progressive Christian to look at progress through different eyes than the dispensationalist. The dispensationalist is suspicious, thinking all things are being taken down the path of destruction and Satan's dominion. Quite to the contrary, progressive Christians see things moving toward dominion and recognize this as God's will. Of course, there are items and points within progress that are negative and even evil, yet the overall plan of God is the advancement of society.

The progressive Christian also understands today's environmental movement differently than the dispensationalist does. The push to care for our environment is in God's heart, and we should expect the corresponding force to increase as we move ahead in time. (Of course, there are some environmentalists who are overly zealous and some elevate the concerns of animals to be equal with people. Such ways of thinking are contrary to Scriptural principles.)

Bringing the Future into Focus

Dispensationalists have little to no reason to work for the preservation of the Earth. Why polish brass on a sinking ship? With that mindset, dispensationalists see the present environmental movement as vain, foolish, and in some ways, opposing the will of God.

Interestingly, the dispensational worldview is less and less attractive to the non-Christian world today, partly because of this lack of concern for the environment. The younger generation has embraced values which elevate environmental concerns. Their views are less compatible with the Dispensational Premillennial worldview of many of their Evangelical Christian parents.

Of course, we do not change our worldview to fit the present culture; however, we do need to go back to Scripture to study, re-evaluate, and see if there is some untruth in our beliefs. This is exactly what I am proposing. Dispensationalism is fundamentally wrong. The progressive worldview is more accurate biblically, and it offers the next generation the Christian worldview which they desperately need.

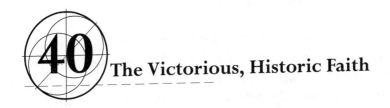

40 The Victorious, Historic Faith

The progressive worldview is based on the belief that God is taking over this world in a progressive fashion

Dispensationalism teaches that Satan is taking over this world in a progressive fashion.

Dispensationalism envisions Satan's kingdom growing until it controls society, all governments, the organized Church, all finances, and finally almost every area of life on this planet. In the end, dispensationalists say Jesus will return to conquer Satan and his kingdom, but until that day, evil will advance continually.

Between now and the return of Jesus, dispensationalists are looking for things to get worse—much worse. Progressive Christians are looking for things to get better—much better.

It is important to know that the historic Church has had an optimistic view throughout most of the last 2,000 years. The negative dispensational view has been predominant only for the last 100 years, and primarily among Evangelical Christians. It is the minority belief historically and in the present worldwide Church. To see this, let's scan Church history and note the hopeful message which has been repeatedly proclaimed.

Bringing the Future into Focus

During the first 250 years after the resurrection of Jesus Christ, the early Christians struggled greatly under persecution. One of the consequences is that today we have only a few preserved writings and no consistent summary of the beliefs of the early Church fathers. However, the renowned teacher Origen (185-254 AD) declared his faith, writing:

> "...every form of worship will be destroyed except the religion of Christ, which will alone prevail. And indeed it will one day triumph, as its principles take possession of the minds of men more and more every day."*

Origen held to this belief in spite of the fact that he was living in incredibly difficult times.

It was not until the Fourth Century that the Roman empire became friendly to Christianity and Church leaders were able to gather together and openly discuss how they understood the Scriptures. In the year 325, over 300 bishops gathered and developed the Nicene Creed, a basic statement of the Christian faith. In addition to this Creed, the bishops discussed many other areas of doctrine. What is significant for our discussion is that they unanimously agreed that the Kingdom of God was to manifest literally on the Earth, and they understood it to be the responsibility of the Church to establish this Kingdom.

---

* Origen, *Against Celsus*, 8:68.

It was Augustine (354-430) who compiled and formulated the most-commonly held Christian beliefs of that time and developed among other things what is called Amillennial eschatology. As we explained earlier, this view sees the Church having the responsibility and authority to establish the Kingdom of God on the Earth (not at some distant point in the future, but now and in every generation). Augustine was confident fully that the Church would succeed.* Although not all Church leaders held to a full confidence in victory, Augustine's Amillennial eschatology dominated the Church's thinking until the late 1700's.

As we study Church history, we can see Christians acting with this Amillennial belief. During the Middle Ages, huge cathedrals, universities, and monasteries were built, some of them taking more than 100 years to complete. Obviously, they were not looking for Jesus to return at any moment. Rather, they were building for the future because they had a theology of victory, not defeat.

Although most of the Church worldwide has remained Amillennial, many Evangelical Christians in America shifted their views to Postmillennialism during the late 1700's. Postmillennialism offers an even more optimistic message than Amillennialism, since it sees the Church victorious to the very end (rather than Satan being released for a short period of havoc at the end). In fact, during the 1800's, Postmillennial views played a major role in many of society's positive advancements, such as the abolition of slavery and

---

* Darrel L. Bock, ed. *Three Views on the Millennium and Beyond*. (Grand Rapids: Zondervan, 1999), 16.

the founding of many universities. At the forefront of such steps were Christian leaders who believed it was their responsibility to change society in an effort to establish the Kingdom of God on the Earth. With this conviction, they set out to make this world a place for the rulership of Jesus Christ.

It was not until the late 1800's that Christians in America began abandoning this hope, along with the associated sense of responsibility.

During the life of the noted English preacher Charles Spurgeon (1834-1894), many Christians began giving up the hope for the victorious Church. Spurgeon held to the optimistic faith, as can be seen in his own words:

> It would be easy to show that at our present rate of progress the kingdoms of this world never could become the kingdom of our Lord and of His Christ. Indeed, many in the Church are giving up the idea of it except on the occasion of the advent of Christ, which as it chimes in with our own idleness, is likely to be a popular doctrine. I myself believe that King Jesus will reign, and the idols be utterly abolished; but I expect the same power which turned the world upside down once will still continue to do it. The Holy Ghost would never suffer the imputation to rest upon His holy name that He was not able to convert the world. *

* Cited in David Chilton, *Paradise Restored: An Eschatology of Dominion.* (Tyler, Texas: Dominion Press, 1999), 129-130.

In spite of such great leaders as Spurgeon, who were in England defending the historic faith, Christians in America moved further toward a defeatist mindset. As dispensationalism crept into American pulpits in the early 1900's, Premillennial eschatology found fertile ground and gradually took root. Then World War I and II erupted, and Christians en masse tried to make sense out of life, resulting in their fuller embracing of the "everything-is-going-downhill" view. During the 1960's, Dispensational Premillennial preaching came to dominate Christian radio and television in America. Evangelists and televangelists especially have been attracted to the Pretribulational, Premillennial endtime scenario, as it offers catastrophic predictions with which excitement is easily stimulated. Over the last 50 years, the negative defeatist worldview has gradually spread to parts of the world being newly evangelized by American Evangelical missionaries.

It is tragic and it is wrong.

It is time for a re-proclamation of the historic, biblical faith.

Conclusion

It will be only a matter of time until the Church of Jesus becomes the most influential entity on the Earth. In truth, it is already the dominant religion worldwide. Christianity shall continue to grow until it is the "largest tree for all the birds of the air to come nest in her branches" (Matt. 13:31-32). There will be a struggle between righteousness and unrighteousness until our Lord returns; however, the Church will continue to advance, shining ever more brightly as a light to the nations.

Dispensationalists will have the most difficult time accepting this optimistic view. Being so immersed in their own endtime visions of coming destruction, they may conclude that I am teaching some new or strange doctrine. In reality, I am proclaiming the historic faith. Of course, I am giving my own understanding of the progressive worldview. However, the foundational optimism which I offer is the worldview of the historic Church. In this I am not offering anything new, but rather I am pleading with the Evangelical community not to fall for the defeatism and negativity of the dispensational worldview with its Premillennial eschatology. Please study, re-evaluate, and then hold to the biblical optimism held by the historic Church.

Bringing the Future into Focus

Allow me to summarize this optimistic, biblical worldview by proclaiming: "Jesus is Lord." It is not enough to interpret this common saying as meaning He will be Lord at some point in the future, nor that He is merely Lord up in heaven right now. Jesus is Lord over heaven and Earth. He sits on a throne and He will continue sitting there until all His enemies are put under His feet. The kingdoms of the Earth are becoming the Kingdoms of our God. A progressive takeover is in process. As surely as God lives, His glory will fill the Earth. Yes, it is true: Jesus is Lord!

Appendix
Recommended Books & Tapes

There are hundreds of books in popular Christian bookstores offering the Dispensational Premillennial view. The list below includes excellent writings presenting other views. Although I do not endorse fully everything written in each of these books, each one will broaden the Christian's understanding of eschatology and offer biblical insights concerning where God is taking the Church in the 21st Century.

Bock, Darrel L., ed. *Three Views on the Millennium and Beyond.* Grand Rapids: Zondervan, 1999.

Chilton, David. *Paradise Restored: An Eschatology of Dominion.* Tyler, Texas: Dominion Press, 1999.

De Mar, Gary. *Last Days Madness: Obsession of the Modern Church.* 3d ed. Atlanta: American Vision, 1997.

Hamon, Bill. *The Eternal Church.* Point Washington, FL: Christian International Publishers, 1981.

Kik, J. Marcellus. *An Eschatology of Victory.* Nutley, NJ: The Presbyterian and Reformed Publishing Co., 1971.

Bringing the Future into Focus

Krupp, Nate. *The Church Triumphant.* Shippensburg, PA: Destiny Image Publishers, 1988.

Murray, Ian. *The Puritan Hope: Revival and the Interpretation of Prophecy.* London: The Banner of Truth Trust, 1971.

Noe, John. *Shattering the Left Behind Delusion.* Bradford, PA: International Preterist Association. 2000.

Pate, C. Marvin, ed. *Four Views on the Book of Revelations.* Grand Rapids: Zondervan, 1998.

Our ministry also produces an album with cassette tapes in which I teach the progressive worldview. These teachings include a clear presentation of how the tribulation which Jesus spoke of in Matthew chapter 24 was fulfilled in 70 AD, and therefore, how we should not expect a Great Tribulation in the future. Request the teaching tape album entitled: *The Progressive Christian Worldview* by Harold R. Eberle. These tapes are available through Winepress Publishing. Information on how to obtain these and other materials follows.

THE COMPLETE WINESKIN (Fourth edition)

The Body of Christ is in a reformation. God is pouring out the Holy Spirit and our wineskins must be changed to handle the new wine. Will the Church come together in unity? Where do small group meetings fit? How does the anointing of God work and what is your role? What is the 5-fold ministry? How are apostles, prophets, evangelists, pastors and teachers going to rise up and work together? This book puts into words what you have been sensing in your spirit. (Eberle's best seller, translated into many languages, distributed worldwide.)

TWO BECOME ONE

Releasing God's Power for Romance, Sexual Freedom and Blessings in Marriage

Kindle afresh the "buzz of love." Find out how to make God's law of binding forces work for you instead of against you. The keys to a thrilling, passionate, and fulfilling marriage can be yours if you want them. This book is of great benefit to pastors, counselors, young singles, divorcees and especially married people. Couples are encouraged to read it together.

THE LIVING SWORD

"The truth shall set you free." So then why does Christian fight Christian over doctrinal issues that seem so clear to each side? Can both be right, or wrong? Learn how Jesus used the Scriptures in His day and then apply those principles to controversial issues currently facing us such as women in the ministry, divorce and remarriage, prosperity, God's plan for our lives,.... What we need is the leading of the Holy Spirit on these subjects. This book will bring the Scriptures alive and set you free.

GOD'S LEADERS FOR TOMORROW'S WORLD

(Revised/expanded edition) You sense a call to leadership in your life, but questions persist: "Does God want me to rise up? Is this pride? Do I truly know where to lead? How can I influence people?" Through a new understanding of leadership dynamics, learn how to develop godly charisma. Confusion will melt into order when you see the God-ordained lines of authority. Fear of leadership will change to confidence as you learn to handle power struggles. Move into your "metron," that is, your God-given authority. You can be all God created you to be!

PRECIOUS IN HIS SIGHT A Fresh Look at the Nature of Man
During the Fourth Century Augustine taught about the nature of man using as his key Scripture a verse in the book of Romans which had been mistranslated. Since that time the Church has embraced a false concept of man which has negatively influenced every area of Christianity. It is time for Christians to come out of darkness! This book, considered by many to be Harold Eberle's greatest work, has implications upon our understanding of sin, salvation, Who God is, evangelism, the world around us and how we can live the daily, victorious lifestyle.

YOU SHALL RECEIVE POWER
Moving Beyond Pentecostal & Charismatic Theology
God's Spirit will fill you in measures beyond what you are experiencing presently. This is not just about Pentecostal or Charismatic blessings. There is something greater. It is for all Christians, and it will build a bridge between those Christians who speak in tongues and those who do not. It is time for the whole Church to take a fresh look at the work of the Holy Spirit in our individual lives. This book will help you. It will challenge you, broaden your perspective, set you rejoicing, fill you with hope, and leave you longing for more of God.

DEAR PASTORS AND TRAVELING MINISTERS,
Here is a manual to help pastors and traveling ministers relate and minister together effectively. Topics are addressed such as ethical concerns, finances, authority, scheduling,…. In addition to dealing with real-life situations, an appendix is included with very practical worksheets to offer traveling ministers and local pastors a means to communicate with each other. Pastors and traveling ministers can make their lives and work much easier by using this simple, yet enlightening, manual.

DEVELOPING A PROSPEROUS SOUL
VOL I: HOW TO OVERCOME A POVERTY MIND-SET
VOL II: HOW TO MOVE INTO GOD'S FINANCIAL BLESSINGS

There are fundamental changes you can make in the way you think which will help release God's blessings. This is a balanced look at the promises of God with practical steps you can take to move into financial freedom. It is time for Christians to recapture the financial arena.

SPIRITUAL REALITIES
Here they are—Harold R. Eberle's series explaining
how the spiritual world and natural world relate.

VOL I: THE SPIRITUAL WORLD AND HOW WE ACCESS IT

Here is a scriptural foundation for understanding the spiritual
world. Learn how to access that world,
touch God, and experience His blessings. Be
aware of the dangers and false manifestations. Release God's power into your life and
the world around us.

VOL II: THE BREATH OF GOD IN US

A study on the nature and origin of the
human spirit, soul, and body. Knowing
God's activities within our being. Understanding the spiritual
energies which God releases in us to think, be physically healthy,
and be sucessful.

VOL. III: ESCAPING DUALISM

Understand how God created you to live as a whole human being:
redeeming the soul, knowing God's will, sanctifying "soul power"
and finding freedom as a child of God. This
book will set you free!

VOL IV: POWERS AND ACTIVITIES OF THE HUMAN SPIRIT

God created you in His image, with His
breath. Discover what this means in relation
to your creative powers, spoken words, dreams, and experiences
in space/time. Here is a Biblical explanation of spiritual
phenomena.

VOL V: SPIRITUAL DYNAMICS BETWEEN PEOPLE

What is going on spiritually between you and the people around
you? Now you can understand spiritual bonds, authority streams,
group consciousness, family dynamics, the
power of free will and covenants.

VOL VI: THE NATURE OF CREATION

The spiritual and natural worlds overlap.
This has profound implications for our un-
derstanding of Creation, the origin of life and death, the nature of
time, laws governing our universe, how our thoughts influence
the natural world, and much more.

MOST RECENT RELEASES

GRACE...THE POWER TO REIGN

The Light Shining from Romans 5-8

We struggle against sin and yearn for God's highest. Yet, on a bad day it is as as if we are fighting with gravity. Questions go unanswered:

- Where is the power to overcome temptations and trials?
- Is God really willing to breathe into us so that these dry bones can live and we may stand strong?

For anyone who ever has clenched his fist in the struggle to live godly, here are the answers. Just as there is a force in the world pushing us to sin, there is a greater force flowing from God which can lift us, transform us, and make us what He wants us to be. It is grace! It is grace which few have grasped, yet, so many have sought desperately. Now you can find it.

BRINGING THE FUTURE INTO FOCUS

An Introduction to the Progressive Christian Worldview

What does the future hold? Will there be peace or war? Are the people of God going to rise up in glory and unity or will they be overcome by apathy and deception? Is Jesus coming for a spotless Bride or is He going to rescue a tattered band of zealots out of a wicked chaotic mess? Where is God taking humanity in the Twenty-First Century?

This book will answer your questions and fill you with hope.

WINEPRESS MINISTRIES

A significant portion of the profit from book sales goes to the support of Christian missions, Bible colleges, charitable work, and orphanages in developing countries around the world. This work is done through the oversight of Winepress Ministries, which is an organization overseen by Harold R. Eberle and a staff of volunteer and paid workers. Winepress Ministries is a ministry based on the belief that God is raising the Church up to a position of unity, maturity, and glory. We believe that the greatest revival the world has ever seen will take place between now and the Second Coming of our Lord Jesus Christ.

The Bible Colleges which Winepress Ministries founds and oversees are growing around the world. These are interdenominational Christian schools graduating several hundred ministers each year. These ministers plant and establish churches primarily in poorer and unreached areas of the world.

If you are looking for something meaningful in which to be involved, we welcome your financial support and we encourage you to join us in helping fulfill the Great Commission to go and make disciples of all nations.

WINEPRESS MINISTRIES
P.O. Box 10653
YAKIMA, WA 98909-1653
E-mail: winepress@nwinfo.net
Web Site: www.winepress.org